ENLIGHTENED AND EMPOWERED

LIVING BY THE SPIRIT

FRED AND SHERRY WHITE

Fountain Gate Publishers
Athens, Georgia USA

TABLE OF CONTENTS

PREFACE

We the Authors (Fred and Sherry White) have been married for over 50 years and have served in some form of ministry for over forty years. Although we wrote this book together, the personal stories are written in Fred's voice.

We both had a call of God on our lives from an early age. Preparation for our calling involved submitting to the Lord's authority, studying the word of God and being taught by anointed ministers. The Lord revealed himself to us in many wonderful ways. We have taught our revelation of him in many different venues in this country and elsewhere. We started teaching the word of God in several congregations, our home and low-income areas. Then we started a mission for homeless people, prostitutes, alcoholics and drug addicts in our city. We financed the mission and other ministry activities on our own until others came alongside us to help. We minister in various congregations, homes, jails, prisons and drug rehabilitation centers. Jesus heals, delivers and sets the people free in these services. He changes the lives of people wherever he sends us. This book was birthed out of praying together, studying the word of God together, and working in the kingdom together.

Purpose of the Book

God's kingdom is manifested by the Spirit operating through the lives of believers. The fruit of the kingdom is righteousness, peace and joy in the Spirit. This book can help readers understand the importance of the Spirit in living a victorious life. It will help believers discover purpose and fulfill destiny. It is filled with foundational kingdom principles and personal experiences to show readers how to apply the principles.

Organization of the Book

The introductory section helps readers discover the importance of the Spirit. The first four chapters cover an introduction to the book, salvation, the infilling of believers with the Spirit, and hearing the Spirit's voice. Salvation and the infilling are fundamental spiritual experiences that open up God's kingdom to believers. The second section shows readers how to draw on various aspects of the Spirit. These chapters cover spiritual fruit, anointing, maturity, and kingdom relationships. The role of the Spirit in producing kingdom fruit and developing kingdom relationships is often overlooked, but the Spirit is critical for believers to fully function in the kingdom. The third section shows how to demonstrate the insight and power of the Spirit. These chapters cover spiritual gifts, strategic prayers and healing, and walking in the Spirit by doing things which seem impossible to the natural mind. It was important for us to have a chapter on healing after discussing the gifts of the Spirit, because a person can be healed even when the gifts are not in operation. The last chapter draws conclusions from every topic covered in the book. It serves as a bridge from the various topics to the lives of the readers. It can help readers identify where they are on their spiritual journey and plan how to move forward in life.

Chapter 1
INTRODUCTION

Great potential lies within every person, but it is hidden from natural eyes. It takes a relationship with God's Spirit to release this potential. His light and power will help you discover and unlock your talents, gifts, and purpose and then propel you into destiny.

Ordinary people are destined to be extraordinary leaders, teachers, parents, employees, etc. Fulfilling destiny is the adventure of a lifetime, and it is the only thing that matters. Release your destiny to start the adventure by believing that you have one. How do you fulfill destiny? This is the most important question that each person has to answer for himself/herself. It is the question that has driven Sherry and me to climb higher and higher on God's holy mountain. "I press on toward the goal for the prize of the upward call of God in Christ Jesus" (Philippians 3:14). Destiny is the reward for pressing on to the goal.

Do not let anyone stop you from taking your mountain. At age 85, Caleb defeated the giants to possess his mountain (Joshua 14-15). Five times people tried to stop us on a plateau and convince us that we had reached the summit of God's mountain. The plateaus involved one of the following.

1. limiting the role of the Spirit to salvation
2. limiting demonstrations of the Spirit's power
3. limiting believers from hearing the Spirit speak
4. limiting believers from fulfilling God's plan
5. limiting believers' authority

These are the same plateaus that are faced by every believer. Many people gather together on a plateau and think that place is all there is of God. People can become comfortable on a plateau and lose sight of the heights of God's mountain. They think spiritual insight and power will come, and they will know how to deal with them. It would have been comfortable to stay with God's people on any of these five plateaus, but the Spirit ignited a fire within us which kept propelling us up higher.

Walking with Jesus in person would be great, but he taught that it's better to have his Spirit dwell in you and fill you to overflowing. Jesus said it is to your advantage that I go away for I will send the Spirit to be your divine helper (John 16:7-11). What is the advantage of living in the presence of the Spirit? The Spirit enlightens and empowers people to become sons of God, to serve him and to glorify him. This book prepares you for living victoriously by the guidance and power of God's Spirit. Filled with foundational Biblical principles, personal experiences and spiritual insights, it will help you soar to in understanding and living.

INTRODUCTION

Each chapter focuses on a specific role of the Spirit and how he enlightens and empowers every believer to fulfill God's purpose and plan in the earth. To be enlightened means to see things the way God sees them, and empowerment is the ability to change things through God's word and accomplish his will.

God is sharing the fresh revelation of his kingdom with his children. It takes spiritual insight to understand the revelation and power to bring it forth. The Spirit is opening the spiritual eyes of believers, so they will see God as he is, partake of his nature, and taste his goodness. Spiritual eyes become open to supernatural things through effective, fervent prayers (Ephesians 1:15-22). When believers' spiritual eyes are open, they will have supernatural power to do the work God has called them to do.

Many Christians do not have the full advantage of the Spirit's light and power. Some receive the Spirit's light without his power. They have a form of godliness but deny its power (2 Timothy 3:5). Others try to operate in the Spirit's power outside of the light. They are living unholy lives and doing unholy deeds, so the revelation they think they have becomes unprofitable and vain. The revelation of God's word without holiness is vanity.

The Spirit's power can be released only when the revealed light of God's word comes. Light is energy, but it has to be harnessed to be productive. Like grass harnesses the energy of sunlight to grow, believers harness the energy of spiritual light by activating and releasing supernatural power to fulfill God's purpose.

Paul encountered Jesus in a great light and received the revelation of his purpose (Acts 9:3-6, 26:13-18). He lived a new life in great power and authority. He healed the sick, cast out demons, and raised the dead. His numerous letters to the churches, which showed his revelation of Jesus Christ, became the core principles of Christian living. First, the light came to him and then supernatural power was released through him to fulfill destiny.

Enlightened by the Spirit

The revelation of the word of God is available to all of God's people. It is a free gift. God sent his word embodied in the flesh of his Son, Jesus. Jesus is the light of the world, and those who follow him will have the light of life (John 8:12). Believers often make decisions in the midst of uncertainties. When the word of God is revealed by his Spirit, it brings light to every situation and makes decisions clear. By following the Spirit, believers can see light instead of darkness. As long as they follow the Spirit, they will stay in the light.

Believers stand on foundation but move in revelation. They cannot move forward without fresh revelation from the Spirit. Life itself comes from the fresh revelation of Jesus as he becomes flesh to believers.

INTRODUCTION

Earnestly desire more revelation of Jesus, and your spirit will be flooded with revelation knowledge and understanding. The scriptures will come alive, and Jesus will become flesh to you. A greater revelation of who Jesus is will become yours. The Spirit will pour out revelation knowledge upon you and reveal God's deep secrets. See Jesus as he is and be just like him.

Empowered by the Spirit

Evil spirits gather around those who are weak, so everyone can benefit from more of God's power. His power will help believers overcome difficult situations and live victoriously. The same power which God used to raise Jesus from the dead is available to believers. With his power, they are able to accomplish more than they could ask or imagine (Ephesians 3:20). The Spirit is the one who makes the power available to believers. In this section, you will learn how to activate the power.

Power Within

Both anointing and grace are available to believers. There are many similarities between anointing and grace, as well as major differences. Both are the power of the Spirit at work in believers. This power comes from the throne of God through the Spirit.

The anointing is the power of God's revealed word. The Spirit reveals the scriptures to believers in order for them to operate in the power of the anointed word. Jesus has always been the word of God, but he did not perform a miracle until the Father revealed him as his beloved Son and anointed him with the Spirit and power (Matthew 3:17; John 1:1). The Spirit anoints the revealed word of God within believers.

Grace is the operational power given to accomplish God's will. "By the grace of God, I am what I am, and his grace toward me did not prove vain; but I labored even more than all of them, yet not I, but the grace of God with me" (1 Corinthians 15:10). Grace flows from the throne of grace to the humble doing God's will. "God is opposed to the proud but gives grace to the humble" (James 4:6). Those who are proud do their own thing by their own strength, so they do not operate in God's power.

The anointing and grace can work together. The power of the anointing is in God's revealed word, and the power of grace is on God's will. When the power of the anointing and the power of grace are combined in a believer's life, there is an ignition and explosion. Great power is released!

Special Endowments

The Spirit can intervene in the lives of believers and unbelievers alike with special endowments of light and power. The gifts of the Spirit are the most notable special endowments (1 Corinthians 12:1-11). The gifts are used for God's glory. The inspiration and verbal gifts enlighten people on the intentions and ways of God.

The power gifts include great faith, the gift of healing, and miraculous power (1 Corinthians 12:9-10 New Living Translation, NLT). The gift of great faith adds God's faith to a believer's measure of faith. People are raised from the dead by greater power than most believers operate in on a regular basis. God's power surging through believers' spirits enables them to walk in the supernatural realm. It will cause them to overcome every obstacle. As people draw on God's power, they will receive his best.

Personal Story about Light and Power

Sherry and I have received many healings in our lives and in the lives of our family. Also, there have been many healings through our ministry. The lame walk, the blind receive sight, and the dead are brought back to life in our ministry.

There was a time when Sherry was having some physical issues with her body. We were praying and believing in her healing, but we had not yet seen the manifestation of her healing. One afternoon as I was praying for her healing, the Spirit instructed us to go to a particular church service that night in another city 40 miles away. There were over two thousand people in that service, and the evangelist had a prophetic word for only four people whom he asked to stand. Sherry was one of the four. He spoke about a chemical imbalance in her body that the Lord was healing. She was healed at that moment. We needed what that evangelist had at that moment for Sherry to be healed. Regardless of how great our understanding and faith are, we need other believers to help us on our journey.

The Challenge

Let the Spirit carry you to new heights in faith, hope, and love.

There are no limits on how high you can soar in God's presence. The Spirit's grace and anointing will show you the way and propel you on your journey of discovery and personal growth. Beginning the journey to new spiritual heights is discussed in the next chapter, and accelerating the pace is discussed in the chapters which follow. Destiny is your reward!

What hinders your spiritual growth?

Chapter 2
BORN OF THE SPIRIT

How has Jesus changed your life? He radically changes things when he becomes a person's savior. By believing Jesus is God's Son, who died and rose again, people experience the new birth and become new creatures (2 Corinthians 5:17). Old things are replaced by new things from God. God's Spirit enters the lives of believers and they are born-again from above, giving them access to the new life with God. They can have new thinking, new ways and new things which bring freedom. Then the Spirit can lead them on their journey here on this earth. In this chapter, you will learn about your new life in God's kingdom.

The ultimate explanation about the new birth comes from Jesus' instructions to Nicodemus (John 3:1-21). God's Spirit recreates the spirit of a believer, making a new creation filled with life where there was only death and darkness. The new creation enters God's kingdom and lives in an environment of love. "We know that we have passed out of death into life because we love the brethren" (1 John 3:14). New creations belong to Jesus Christ because the new birth was made possible through his death and resurrection. Those who belong to

Christ are the spiritual descendants of Abraham and heirs of God's promised blessings (Galatians 3:29).

The new birth involves both enlightenment and empowerment. Those who are born again have been enlightened about the need for a savior and about Jesus being the only way to God. They have received the right and power of God to become children of God. The new birth gives believers access to far more enlightenment and empowerment than the new birth itself. After the new birth, believers can be filled with God's Spirit, operate in the gifts of the Spirit, and walk in the Spirit.

God's Wind

The Spirit is God's wind and breath. Both the Hebrew word for Spirit (ruwach) and the Greek word for Spirit (pneuma) mean wind and breath. The Spirit moves over the earth like the wind. "The earth was formless and void, and darkness was over the surface of the deep, and the Spirit of God was moving over the surface of the waters" (Genesis 1:2). The Spirit was prepared to create whatever God desired and spoke out of his mouth.

All life comes from the breath of God. "Then the Lord God formed man of dust from the ground, and breathed into his nostrils the breath of life; and man became a living being" (Genesis 2:7). This life is natural, not spiritual. Even so, the life which God imparted to Adam is so far-reaching that all humans are his natural descendants. Jesus moved among the people like the wind. He came, he ministered and then he was gone. He breathed on his disciples, and they received his life (John 20:20). When God's wind blows on believers, they receive his light and his power to fulfill destiny.

The Spirit of the Believer

Those who are born of the Spirit are the wind and are not to be confined to men's thinking and their traditions. They move like the wind by following the leading of the Spirit. "The wind blows where it wishes and you hear the sound of it, but do not know where it comes from and where it is going; so is everyone who is born of the Spirit" (John 3:8). Those who are born of the Spirit are given a spirit of freedom to move like the wind.

The spirit of a believer is recreated by the Spirit and adopted into the family of God. What does this mean? First, the spirit of a believer desires the things of God. We have received God's Spirit who produces sonship by which we call him our Father (Romans 8:15). The spirit will pursue heavenly things (Colossians 3:1-2). The spirit yearns for fellowship with the Lord.

Second, the main purpose of the spirit of a believer is to yield fruit for the Lord. This fruit includes love, joy, peace and the other fruit of the Spirit (Galatians 5:22-23). When believers become renewed in their minds, they are able to separate their spirits from their souls and become fruitful.

11

Third, the spirit of a believer needs to be liberated to fulfill destiny. People who experience the new birth still have to be loosed from all the things keeping them in bondage, such as old thinking, opinions of others, fears and teachings from man. It takes God's Spirit to free and energize the spirit of a believer. The Spirit brings freedom (2 Corinthians 3:17). He frees the spirits of believers as they fellowship with him.

It takes the anointed word of God to separate the spirit from the soul and the spiritual from the natural (Hebrews 4:12). Prayer is critical for releasing the spirit of a believer. Believers can operate a vibrant prayer life by studying and applying the prayers that are recorded in the word of God. Just repeating these prayers will not ensure the spirit of a believer will be brought forth in its fullness. Asking the Father for his guidance through the Spirit will help identify strategic and effective prayers. Reliance on the Spirit is needed for the full development of the spirit of a believer.

New Life

The essential supernatural experience is the new birth or salvation. It imparts spiritual life and opens the door to all other major supernatural experiences. The new birth brings life to a spirit of death and darkness. The tremendous price that Jesus, the Son of God, paid on the cross for salvation makes it the greatest gift that anyone could receive. It is a free gift which should never be neglected.

As long as believers remain an open vessel to God's spiritual life, they can walk in his blessings. Many people want God to change their circumstances and bless them, without realizing that he is at work within them changing their lives. Spiritual life can flow through every area of a believer's life. The flow of spiritual life begins at its source, Jesus Christ (John 1:1-4, 10:10). The Spirit imparts spiritual life into a person's spirit with the new birth. It is the Spirit who gives life (John 6:63). God works from the inside out, changing the very core of a believer, his/her spirit or heart. "Above all else, guard your heart, for everything you do flows from it" (Proverbs 4:23 New International Version´, NIV).

Spiritual life is first in a believer's heart or spirit and can flow from there to other areas. A thankful heart is an open vessel for spiritual life and God's blessings. After experiencing the new birth, a believer's soul can be saved with the anointed word. "Putting aside all filthiness and all that remains of wickedness, in humility receive the word implanted, which is able to save your souls" (James 1:21). The spirit is the container and when it overflows from the blessings of heaven it will pour into the soul and then onto the body and natural realm.

Personal Stories about the New Birth

Both Sherry and I had serious problems as children that we had to overcome. We overcame them with determination and self-reliance. As a result, we became strong-willed and independent individuals who would try to succeed with or without God. But God intervened in our lives. At the age of nine, Sherry wrestled one night with the Lord before giving her heart to him. For months after my friends accepted the Lord, I resisted him before giving my heart to him and being born again at age 13. My spirit became alive to spiritual things, but I was not prepared for the spiritual battle that followed. My carnal mind quickly prevailed, and I returned to the old ways of thinking and acting.

After we were born again, we truly committed our lives to the Lord and would serve him all our lives. We loved the Lord, loved going to church services to hear about him and loved being with his people. In all the church services which we attended for several years, we were told nothing about God's Spirit. Consequently, we remained carnally minded for a period of several years.

We were living on a broad plateau of God's mountain with multitudes of people who focused continually on salvation and nothing more. We received the power to become children of God and wanted others to be saved because that message was preached over and over again. This is the first plateau on which we were trapped, but it was not the last. We were powerless to move beyond salvation because we never heard of God's Spirit and power.

Our children were sick and dying and our marriage was broken, and we were powerless to do anything. Like all our friends we looked to doctors and other natural ways out of our problems, but we found no answers. Rather than see our children perish and let our marriage end in divorce, Sherry decided to commit suicide. She asked the Lord whether that was all he had for her for she was ready to go to him. Is there more than the new birth?

The Challenge

Be a free spirit full of new life, light, and power.
As a born-again believer, you are a spirit rather than a living soul. Your spirit is alive to spiritual things. Do not let people define you and set limits on you. Study God's word yourself to free your thinking and see yourself as God sees you. Build a strong relationship with God's Spirit to open your spiritual eyes.

Is there more for you in this life than salvation?

Chapter 3
FILLED WITH THE SPIRIT

Are you continually filled with the Spirit's power? One of the most important things God uses to affect lives is his power. He is able to do great things in our lives according to the power within us (Ephesians 3:20). Years ago, we felt hopeless and powerless to cope with the issues we faced in life. Sherry wanted to end her life when she saw no hope and no future, but the Lord began to show us that there is more to life when we are filled with his Spirit and power.

While some people try to limit or reject his power in their lives, others energize and activate the power within them. Those who truly release themselves to the Spirit and his power will see God do great things in their lives and the lives of others. In this chapter, you will explore the process and benefits of being filled with the Spirit and power.

Introducing the Infilling of the Spirit

Believers can be filled with the Spirit after receiving salvation. Jesus imparted salvation to his disciples when he breathed on them and said, "Receive the Holy Spirit" (John 20:22). Later,

Jesus told these same disciples to tarry until they received the Spirit (Acts 1:4-8). On the day of Pentecost, these disciples and others were filled with the Spirit and fire. "They were all filled with the Holy Spirit and began to speak with other tongues, as the Spirit was giving them utterance" (Acts 2:4). This was the initial fulfillment of John the Baptist's prophecy concerning Jesus: "He will baptize you with the Holy Spirit and fire" (Matthew 3:11). The disciples were baptized in the Spirit and equipped with the power of the Spirit to glorify the Father among the nations.

The transforming power of the Spirit is released in believers when they are saved, but it is intensified when they are filled with the Spirit. Christ lives in all those who believe, but it takes the power of the Spirit to let Christ live through them. "I have been crucified with Christ; and it is no longer I who live, but Christ lives in me" (Galatians 2:20). This transforming power allows the manifestation of Christ to be evident in the lives of believers.

In the Old Testament, the filling of the Spirit was given sovereignly by God, so it was not available to all. The filling of the Spirit was related to wisdom and the ability to serve in some particular area. Joseph was selected to rule in Egypt because of the Spirit and wisdom within him (Genesis 41:38-40). Joshua, who was filled with the Spirit, was chosen to succeed Moses as the leader of Israel (Numbers 27:18). The Spirit also gave God's people special skills to make priestly garments and to build the tabernacle (Exodus 28:3, 35:30-35). The Spirit came on men to deliver Israel from their enemies and serve as judges over them. The Spirit gave Samson superhuman strength.

Why be filled with the Spirit and speak in tongues? When believers pray in tongues by the Spirit, they communicate with God and build up their faith (1 Corinthians 14:2; Jude 1:20). Praying in the Spirit is the last piece of powerful prayer armor (Ephesians 6:18). All of these reasons explain why believers need to be filled with the Spirit and pray in tongues.

In the New Testament, the Spirit was given to those who yielded themselves to God. The filling of the Spirit enhances the spiritual development of the believer. A few manifestations of the Spirit were mentioned during the period of time leading up to the birth of Jesus. The Spirit moved on Zechariah, Elizabeth, and Simeon. John the Baptist was filled with the Spirit from his mother's womb (Luke 1:15). The full outpouring of the Spirit began after the ascension of Jesus to heaven (Acts 2:1-4).

Believers are challenged and commanded to be filled with the Spirit. "Don't be drunk with wine, which will ruin your life, but be filled with the Spirit" (Ephesians 5:18 Easy-to-Read Version, ERV). Like drinking wine excessively can affect everything in a person's life, the infilling of the Spirit can influence every aspect of a believer's life. Believers can be continually filled with the Spirit. "The disciples were continually filled with joy and with the Holy Spirit" (Acts

13:52). Continually being filled with the Spirit makes a believer more aware of the things of God. It opens up gates to the supernatural realm.

How to Be Filled with the Spirit

Preparing the heart with humility is a critical aspect of receiving the Spirit and worshipping the Lord. A group of Jesus' disciples met in the Upper Room with one mind and one purpose continually devoting themselves to prayer in anticipation of the outpouring of the Spirit (Acts 1:14). Then the Spirit came into their midst with a sound of heaven and baptized all of them with power and fire. It is the power and fire that enables believers to change their lives, their ways, their thinking and propel them into their destinies.

There are many ways to receive the infilling of the Spirit. In every case, faith to receive is involved. Believers can ask and receive the manifestation of the Spirit themselves without help from anyone else. On the day of Pentecost, the disciples met in agreement with God and received the infilling of the Spirit without assistance from man.

Believers can lay hands on one another to be filled with the Spirit. Peter and John were sent by the believers in Jerusalem to witness the revival that was occurring with Philip. They laid their hands on new believers to receive the Spirit, and the new believers were filled with the Spirit (Acts 8:14-17).

Five Benefits of Being Filled with the Spirit

When believers are filled with the Spirit, God covers them and abides in them with his fullness. All of his nature is infused, intensified and activated to its full capacity. His love and compassion flow over them. Five important effects of the infilling of the Spirit are discussed below.

1. Know God's Ways

Being filled with the Spirit helps believers become aware of his presence and power in them. The Spirit takes the things of the Father and the Son and shows them to believers (John 16:15). Those who are sensitive to the Spirit live in a way that honors and respects his presence. They spend time in his presence by praying with their spirits and singing with their spirits (1 Corinthians 14:15). They allow God's Spirit to express himself through their actions without grieving him or quenching his fire (Ephesians 4:30; 1 Thessalonians 5:19). As believers allow the Spirit to move through them, their sensitivity to spiritual things will increase.

2. Fellowship with God

As believers pray in the Spirit, they become one with God. The lines of communication are opened, and they can speak to him without interference from the devil because he cannot interrupt the heavenly message.

21

Praying in the spirit language is not a product of the natural mind but an operation of God's Spirit. When believers pray in their spirit language, their spirits are praying (1 Corinthians 14:14). While their spirits pray, their minds become quiet. This is particularly important when their thoughts are scattered and anxious about something. When believers pray in the Spirit, they are praying God's perfect will and increasing their faith. Then they can be confident that they are changing situations.

3. Be Creative

All creativity is given by the Creator for his glory and his purpose. It is a supernatural ability that is released, enhanced and enriched by praying in the Spirit. Believers have creativity inside of them. Many times, people do not know how to release their creativity until they are filled with the Spirit. The Spirit will reveal things to come (John 16:13). The Spirit helps believers creatively visualize potential, possibilities and capabilities in people, ministry, and other things.

Many of our friends are artists, musicians, craftsmen, designers, developers, and inventors. Several of these people had special God-given abilities before they knew Jesus as Savior. After being born again and filled with the Spirit, their abilities were enhanced. Others did not realize they had special abilities until they were born again and filled with the Spirit. The Spirit helped them identify and develop their special abilities. The Spirit gave them songs to sing, images to paint, innovative designs, inventions, and other creative ideas. Their creative ideas have blessed them and many, many others.

4. Release Spiritual Gifts

There are many different types of spiritual gifts, but they all come from God through Christ and the Spirit. These gifts are developed in their fullness through the infilling of the Spirit. These gifts are to be used as the Spirit wills and for the glory of God. Some spiritual gifts can be seen in each person. The three groups of spiritual gifts listed in God's word are discussed in this section. There are gifts of service such as teaching, encouraging, giving, and hospitality (Romans 12:6-8; I Peter 4:10-11). Then there are gifts that demonstrate God's power and presence. These include wisdom, knowledge, faith, miracles and the gifts of tongues and interpretation. All the gifts are to build up the body of Christ and to bring his body into its glorious state.

Ministry gifts are given to mature God's people and prepare them for service (Ephesians 4:11; 1 Corinthians 12:27-31). These gifts include the apostles, prophets, pastors, evangelists, and teachers. Apostles bring authority, prophets bring direction, pastors bring spiritual food and nurturing, teachers show God's ways, and evangelists share the good news with those who do not know Jesus. These diverse roles help grow, strengthen, and unify the glorious body of Christ.

5. Overcome Evil

Being filled with the Spirit enables believers to destroy the works of the devil strategically and effectively as Jesus did. "The Son of God appeared for this purpose, to destroy the works of the devil" (1 John 3:8). By the Spirit, believers can enter into enemy territory with power and push back the devil's forces. They wrestle not with flesh and blood but with rulers of the darkness (Ephesians 6:12). Believers go into the supernatural realm and fight the good fight of faith by praying in the Spirit and receiving God's wisdom and power.

Personal Stories on Being Filled with the Spirit

When Sherry and I prayed together to receive the Spirit, we were sitting in our home. No one else was there to pray for us. Sherry began to pray with her spirit through God's Spirit within her, but her new language initially sounded like a turkey gobbling. I did not think I had been filled with the Spirit because I did not feel anything special. A few days later in a church service, I prayed with my spirit for the first time as God's Spirit moved on me. Then I knew I had received the gift of tongues for public ministry, as well as my personal prayer language. Even though I did not feel anything special when I asked to be filled with the Spirit, my prayer had been answered. Never again would I doubt that I had been filled with the Spirit.

After being filled with the Spirit, we started attending church services with others who had experienced the infilling of the Spirit. In these services, the Spirit was openly discussed. The people knew about the Spirit's power, but there was no demonstration of his power. Multitudes of people appeared to be satisfied on a plateau of God's holy mountain where the infilling of the Spirit had been experienced but his power was not demonstrated. Many on this level thought they had an advantage over those who were born of the Spirit but not filled with the Spirit. This was the second plateau on which we were trapped. There was much in those church services to attract people, including lively praise and special programs. However, mere performances do not compare with the demonstration of the power. We wanted to see the demonstration of God's power.

The Challenge

Stay continually filled with the Spirit's great power.
Believers are continually filled with the Spirit when they are praying in their spirit language and being led by the Spirit. It is a choice that each believer has to make. Being filled and continually refilled with the Spirit gives you access to great power.

How can you release God's great power in your own life and in the world?

Chapter 4
HEAR THE SPIRIT'S VOICE

God's Spirit leads people to the truth and freedom, but how can they follow the Spirit if they do not hear his voice? If they are led by the Spirit, they are free from the control of the sinful nature and control of the law (Galatians 5:16-18). Many do not hear the Spirit because they expect him to speak like a man, but he is a spirit and speaks in ways which are mysterious to the carnal mind. While the Spirit can speak to babes in Christ, his voice is heard best by trained spiritual ears and understood best by renewed minds. Spiritual ears and a renewed mind are products of spiritual growth. Understanding how to hear the Spirit will help renew your mind and train your spiritual ears. In this chapter, you will learn how to hear and recognize the voice of the Spirit.

Introducing the Spirit's Voice

The Spirit will speak to you. He speaks what he hears from the Father (John 16:13). His message is about Jesus and leads believers into all the truth. Hearing the voice of the Spirit demystifies the will of God. By the Spirit, God reveals his "wisdom, a mystery that has been hidden" (1 Corinthians 2:7-10).

The Spirit's words are not carved in stone like the law which God gave Moses. Instead, his words are like the gentle whisper through which God spoke to Elijah. After a wind, earthquake, and fire there was the sound of a breeze, "and through this breeze, a gentle, quiet voice entered into Elijah's ears" (1 Kings 19:11-12 Holy Bible, Voice™, VOICE). The Spirit speaks words like a gentle blowing. His words come like thoughts into a person. They are often fleeting thoughts that have to be grasped quickly before they leave a person's thinking. The person will know the Spirit's words are not his/her own thoughts. The Spirit's words will be consistent with written scriptures.

The Spirit can communicate in various ways. His words might be heard as a still, small voice within a person or a knowing witness in a person's spirit. They might be heard through dreams and visions. Four important ways he communicates are discussed below.

1. Calling

The Spirit's words that reveal a person's calling are full of energy. His energy may be manifested in unique ways, making a person's calling particularly memorable. Moses received his calling to be a ruler and a deliverer from a voice in a burning bush (Acts 7:30-34). Jeremiah's calling as a prophet was like a fire shut up in his bones (Jeremiah 20:9). As the Spirit reveals a person's calling, he brings light and life to a specific scripture or instruction. When believers are touched by the Spirit as they hear their calling, they may be moved in their hearts to activate their calling by praying and studying God's word.

When I heard the Lord's voice by the Spirit call me to the ministry, it felt like a jolt of electricity hit me. I jumped up and ran from one room in my house to another, trying to comprehend with my mind what I heard with my spirit. It was as if the Lord spoke to me in an audible voice. I was sure others could have heard it if they had been nearby. It happened many years ago, but the memory of it is still very vivid. Although only a few words were spoken, the message exploded inside me. I knew it encompassed much more than the words which I heard. Then I began to prepare myself to answer my calling to minister. Since then, Sherry and I have been spreading the gospel of the kingdom to the nations.

2. Direction

The Spirit's directions are clear. The Spirit told Philip "Go up and join this chariot" (Acts 8:29). By these instructions, Philip knew where to go and what to do. While the prophets and teachers at Antioch were seeking the Lord, the Spirit said, "Set apart for me Barnabas and Saul for the work to which I have called them" (Acts 13:2). Only Barnabas and Saul were selected from these prophets and teachers. The Spirit gives believers time to consider their choices, so they can make the best decisions.

3. Correction

The Spirit's corrections are indisputable. He speaks with low, authoritative tones to bring correction. When he brings correction, there is no question about his meaning. He spoke twice to Peter about his own false doctrine so there would be no question about his meaning (Acts 11:9). Correction is not enjoyable at the time, but it brings peace to those who do what is right (Hebrews 12:11). I have argued with the Spirit on different occasions without any success. It is best to follow the Spirit by making any changes he wants.

4. Comfort

The God of all comfort operates through his Spirit to comfort his people (2 Corinthians 1:3; Acts 9:31). The Spirit speaks in soft, gentle tones to bring comfort. Different tones help people understand the meaning of what is being spoken (Galatians 4:20). Believers are able to comfort others with the same comfort which they have received from the Spirit. In a time of my grief, the Spirit comforted me with gentle words about Christ's love for me. Now, I am able to help comfort others.

Three Keys to Hearing the Spirit's Voice

The Spirit gives people direct access to God's presence, guidance and wisdom. He is watching, listening and speaking to people. They are often unprepared and too busy to listen to what the Spirit is speaking. You can prepare yourself to hear the Spirit by developing a relationship with him, becoming sensitive to his voice and following his guidance. Here are three important keys to hearing the Spirit's voice.

1. Renewal of the Mind

Before experiencing the new birth, people were slaves to sin. The Spirit takes people from having a slave mentality into sonship and freedom. "You have not received a spirit of slavery leading to fear again, but you have received a spirit of adoption as sons" (Romans 8:15). A radical change in thinking is required to transform a slave mentality to sonship. It takes the light and power of the Spirit to renew a person's mind from slavery to sonship.

See things from God's perspective rather than your own circumstances and hurts. The same attitude and mind of Christ Jesus can direct your thoughts through the word of God and his Spirit (Philippians 2:5). Renew your mind to the word of God (Ephesians 4:23). Stop thinking like people in the world. Put off the old corrupt way of thinking which includes such things as doubt, fear, self-centeredness, and bitterness, and begin to think like God. The carnal mind is an enemy of God, but a renewed mind is in agreement with God. Believers are transformed to be like Christ by renewing their minds.

2. Prayer

Prayer is the starting point for a conversational friendship with the Spirit. "The Friend, the Holy Spirit whom the Father will send at my request, will make everything plain to you" (John 14:26 MSG). The Spirit is the friend who will never leave you, and he wants you to be his friend. Prayer is simply two friends talking together. You speak to him and you listen to him as he speaks to you. Pray regularly, and always be open to hearing from him. When you do not know how to pray, ask for the Spirit's help. He is here to help you.

3. Fellowship with the Spirit

Lay aside the things which burden you and take time for sharing and intimate fellowship with the Spirit. Fellowship with the Spirit joins you with him, prepares you to think like God, and enables you to love others. Paul prayed, "The fellowship of the Holy Spirit be with you all" (2 Corinthians 13:14). Be attentive to the still, small voice of the Spirit rather than the many loud, driving voices of the world. The Spirit can speak to you as you sleep and when you are awake. As you fellowship with the Spirit, you will have a witness in your spirit to the plan and purpose for which you have been called.

Hindrances to Hearing the Spirit's Voice

There are some common hindrances to hearing the voice of the Spirit. Unbelievers generally do not hear his voice, because their spirits have not been regenerated to the things of heaven. Only those people who belong to the Lord are given the promise of hearing his voice.

Many people have not heard the voice of the Spirit because their ears have not been attentive. Those who are settled and those who are comfortable and complacent with their praise and knowledge have difficulty hearing the Spirit. Those people have taken God's word within the context of their own thinking and perverted his plan.

There are many voices competing for attention. The spirit man, the old man, and the devil want to be heard. Conscience is the voice of the spirit man, distinguishing between right and wrong. When believers hear a voice from within saying a particular action is wrong, they are hearing their conscience, not God's Spirit. People are right with God when their spirit man does not condemn them, so they can ask God anything confidently. Fleshly desire is the voice of the old man. Cravings for drugs, alcohol and junk food are a few of the fleshly desires. The scriptures provide a more extensive list of fleshly desires (Galatians 5:19-21). The devil's voice is condemning and driving people to make quick and inappropriate decisions. He tries to force people into desperate and hopeless situations.

When people know what God wants them to do but they do the opposite, they harden their hearts to hearing from the Spirit. Following the leading of the Spirit keeps believers' hearts sensitive to the Spirit. Many think they are following the voice of the Spirit when they are following man. They have not developed a love for the truth. A love of the truth will keep them following the Spirit on the path of righteousness.

Tuning Spiritual Ears to Hear the Spirit

The sound of the Spirit's voice is on a supernatural frequency, which is outside the range heard by natural ears. When spiritual people heard words from heaven, the natural people around them could not understand what was said (John 12:28-29). The natural man does not perceive the things of the Spirit of God (1 Corinthians 2:14). The Spirit's words are received by the spirit man and transmitted to the mind.

God's Spirit speaks to man's spirit on a spirit-to-spirit basis. "God is a spirit, and those who worship him must worship in spirit and truth" (John 4:24). When David was in the spirit, he understood Christ was his Lord (Matthew 22:42-44). Religious people called Christ the Son of David, but in the spirit, David exalted him as Lord. Believers know things in the spirit and by God's Spirit which the natural mind does not understand. "You are not in the flesh but in the spirit if indeed the Spirit of God dwells in you" (Romans 8:9). John was in the spirit when he heard a voice instruct him to write down a vision

34

and then send it to the churches (Revelation 1:10-11). The term in the spirit means a person is in spiritual communion with God.

The way to begin experiencing the Spirit is to become attentive to his voice. As the Spirit reveals God's word, believers will be made alive in Jesus. Enter the rest of the Lord by believing his word. Stay in his rest by consistently following the Spirit.

Hearing the Spirit leads to righteousness, peace, and joy (Romans 14:17, 15:13). Choose the path for which you have an inward peace. "Depart from evil and do good; seek peace and pursue it" (Psalm 34:14).

The Lord is inviting his people to move to a higher level in him. Your hearing has to be fine-tuned as you go higher up the mountain of the Lord. Those who are close to him will hear his Spirit's voice and move with his voice. Listen closely to the voice of his Spirit. Many of God's people who know that he speaks are content to let others tell them what he is saying. As long as we were depending on pastors and prophets to tell us what the Spirit was saying, we were trapped spiritually. This was the third plateau on which we were trapped, along with many others. It would have been comfortable to stay at that level and appear to be spiritual. But we had to keep climbing higher by hearing from the Spirit ourselves.

Personal Story on Learning to Hear the Spirit

Sherry trained herself to hear the Spirit by relying on one of the Lord's promises to us. She could hear Jesus' voice because she was one of his sheep. Jesus said, "My sheep hear my voice" (John 10:27). Many times, she would repeat to Jesus, "I am one of your sheep, and I hear your voice". Over time, she became more and more sensitive to the Spirit.

The Challenge

Develop a conversational friendship with the Spirit that will enable you to hear him speaking to you regularly.

Tune your spiritual ears to hear the Spirit's voice. Be attentive to the guidance of the Spirit and quick to respond to his leading. Let the Spirit be part of everything in your life. His guidance will show you the way. His presence will fill you with peace and joy to enable you to do what needs to be done.

How do you take notice of what the Spirit says to you and apply it to your life?

Fruit contains the seed of life. Each piece of fruit from a tree has within it the seed of life to produce many orchards for generation after generation. Spiritual fruit, such as love, joy, and righteousness, contains the seed of life to produce multitudes of fruit bearers from one generation to another. As a fruit bearer offers fruit to people, they will be able to taste the Lord and see he is good. They will not be able to resist the love of God: "Love never fails" (1 Corinthians 13:8). Believers can bring forth the fruit of repentance, light, righteousness, and the kingdom to name just a few. In this chapter, you will learn how to be fruitful in every area of your life.

Introducing Spiritual Fruit

Spiritual fruit is relational in nature, being produced through divine relationships and poured out in interpersonal relationships. This fruit is produced from strong relationships with the Father, his Son and his Spirit (John 15:1-8). Jesus Christ is the first fruits and the source of fruit in believers as they share his life. "I am the vine, you are the branches; he who abides in me and I in him, he bears much fruit, for apart from me you can do nothing" (John 15:5). The Father takes care of the spiritual vineyard in the hearts of believers, and their fruitfulness glorifies him. The Spirit is the fruit producer. This fruit is not produced by the will or works of the believer but by the Spirit. When the Spirit comes into a person's life, he begins to clean out the heart and plant the seed of God's word. "The love of God has been poured out within our hearts through the Holy Spirit who was given to us" (Romans 5:5). Then the seed begins to grow and produce a harvest of fruit in the hearts of believers. The most well-known spiritual fruit is the fruit of the Spirit, but there are many other types of fruit listed in the word of God.

Love, joy, peace and other spiritual fruit flow through a believer to those with whom he/she comes in contact. A believer's spiritual fruit can benefit many others as it is freely shared with them. The fruit builds relationships and holds relationships together.

Offer people wine to taste, and they will consider its appearance, scents, and flavors. Offer them spiritual fruit to taste, and they will consider these same attributes and others, as well. "We are a fragrance of Christ to God among those who are being saved and among those who are perishing" (2 Corinthians 2:15). The fragrance of believers is perceived differently by different people. The best fruit will awaken their natural and spiritual senses and draw them to Christ by the Spirit.

The term spiritual refers to a dimension higher than this world. While the things of this world have three dimensions, spiritual fruit comes from a higher, supernatural dimension. The love of Christ is the fourth dimension outside of time and space. Paul prayed the Lord's holy people would "grasp how wide and long and high and deep is the love of Christ" (Ephesians 3:18 NIV).

Spiritual fruit cannot be understood by intellectual or carnal minds. Christ's love is greater than anyone can understand fully (Ephesians 3:19). God's peace is too great to understand. "The peace of God, which surpasses all comprehension, will guard your hearts and your minds in Christ Jesus" (Philippians 4:7). It takes the Spirit to reveal the hidden things about the fruit.

Fruit fills every aspect of a fruit bearer's life. It grows in the heart and spills over into the soul and kingdom. Changes in behavior and situations begin first in the heart. Fruit is grown in believers' hearts by the Spirit. As they renew their minds to the anointed word of God, their souls produce fruit. Then their efforts in the kingdom are fruitful.

Fruit of Repentance

The New Testament begins with the account of a great spiritual awakening and calls for the fruit of repentance. Many people came to hear John the Baptist and to be cleansed of their sins through water baptism (Matthew 3:1-11). John called for them to bring forth the fruit of repentance (Matthew 3:8). He explained this fruit involved a selfless attitude and kindness to others (Luke 3:10-15). Since the Messiah had not yet fulfilled his mission, the changes John called for were aimed at the soul rather than the spirit. Only after the death and resurrection of Jesus could the spirits of men become alive. Hence the fruit of repentance which John called for was fruit in the soul.

Repentance is the humble response of a person convicted of sin by the work of the Spirit. The Spirit "will convict the world concerning sin and righteousness and judgment" (John 16:8). Repentance involves a person's willingness to change his/her way of thinking and acting. It is the reconciling gift of God's grace, which draws people close to him. It begins with a change in the way a person thinks and leads to a change in actions so that earlier offenses are not repeated. It relates to ceasing from sin against God and resolving to obey him. Godly sorrow is the catalyst which leads to repentance and permanent changes in the way people think and act (2 Corinthians 7:9).

Knowing who you are in Christ helps you know right from wrong. Take off the old man, and put on the new man which gives life in Christ (Ephesians 4:23-24). Your attitude becomes like his. You do not struggle with flesh and blood, even your own flesh. "For our struggle is not against flesh and blood, but against...the spiritual forces of wickedness in the heavenly places" (Ephesians 6:12). Flesh cannot control the fleshly sinful nature, such as overeating or drug addictions. Saying you are not going to overeat or take drugs keeps you in the flesh. Repent and focus on who you are in Christ. Repentance helps you to turn from the fleshly struggle and into true humility which relies on the Spirit to put down the flesh. Ask the Spirit to help rule your flesh.

Renewal of the mind is critical to repentance. Otherwise, a person will go back to the same old offenses. A radical change in thinking is needed for people to be free from the old way of life and united with Jesus in a new life. Thinking like God is radical to the world, but we have been given the mind of Christ (1 Corinthians 2:16). It's radical to give when the natural mind wants to hoard up, and it's radical to love those whom others despise. As you renew your mind to the word of God and truly repent, you will be in a position to produce new fruit abundantly. The fruit of repentance will bring lasting changes.

Fruit of the Spirit

Several kinds of fruit can be in the heart of a believer, but love holds everything together. "Put on love, which is the perfect bond of unity" (Colossians 3:14). The fruit of the Spirit is love, joy, peace, patience, kindness, goodness, faithfulness, gentleness, and self-control (Galatians 5:22-23). Even in difficult situations, believers can demonstrate kindness and faithfulness which only come through the Spirit. They can reflect the goodness of God and his patience towards all people. There is a specific fruit for every situation. The Spirit will minister peace in the midst of storms and joy in times of mourning. These kinds of fruit are available for all those who follow the Spirit and live in the Spirit.

The love of Christ is different from all of the natural forms of love such as physical and romantic love. His love is spiritual and unconditional. Only those who have Christ living inside them can walk in the love of Christ. Worldly people might have good character traits, such as being caring, patient, and happy. However, they cannot produce spiritual fruit.

Jesus demonstrated the greatest love by his death on the cross. "Greater love has no one than this, that one lay down his life for his friends" (John 15:13). He commanded his disciples to demonstrate this same great love. "This is my commandment, that you love one another, just as I have loved you" (John 15:12). His disciples are predestined to be conformed to his image, which is the family image of love. It is not the outward appearance but the inner man or heart which takes on this image of the greatest love. The greatest love is God's excellent way of life (1 Corinthians 12:31-13:7). The greatest love is humble, kind, forgiving and believing.

Fruit of the Kingdom

God's kingdom and righteousness are the most important things for believers to pursue. "Seek first his kingdom and his

(Matthew 6:33). Nothing else compares to the kingdom and
righteousness. The kingdom is built by fruit bearers with
spiritual fruit that lasts. The fruit of the kingdom is
righteousness, peace, and joy in the Spirit (Romans 14:17).
The kingdom will be taken away from those who do not
produce kingdom fruit and given to those bearing its fruit
(Matthew 21:43). Building on anything other than kingdom
fruit will not last.

God's peace can replace trouble in the hearts of believers.
A mind focused on the Spirit will find full life and complete
peace (Romans 8:6 VOICE). His peace allows you to live with
a sense that all things are coming together for good (Romans
8:28). When his peace rules a believer's heart and soul, it
becomes evident in their lives.

A glorious joy fills the hearts of those who enter the
presence of the Lord. "In your presence is the fullness of joy"
(Psalm 16:11). In his presence problems fade away, obstacles
vanish and victory is revealed. Believers respond to the
goodness of the Lord with joy radiating out of their hearts. Joy
comes from doing the Father's will. It was a joy which brought
Jesus to the cross and beyond. He endured the cross for the joy
set before him (Hebrews 12:2). Jesus saw his purpose, fulfilled
his destiny, and was glad. Likewise, believers obey the Father's
will and fulfill destiny for the joy of it, not for its reward. The

sound of joy signifies victory. Joy is a supernatural force responding to the goodness of the Lord.

God offers righteousness in Christ to all who believe. Christ was made to be sin so we might be made the righteousness of God in him (2 Corinthians 5:21). Although his righteousness is available to all, some do not live righteously. Those who do what is right according to the word of God are righteous (1 John 3:7).

A righteous path is laid out for each believer to discover purpose and fulfill destiny. Other paths might appear appealing, but God's purpose for an individual is found only on this one path. "Many are the plans in a person's heart, but it is the Lord's purpose that prevails" (Proverbs 19:21 NIV). The righteous path for purpose and destiny is the one which shines as brightly as the early morning light. "The path of the righteous is like the light of dawn, that shines brighter and brighter until the full day" (Proverbs 4:18). The light of God's word and his Spirit show the way.

God's purpose is a mystery to be revealed by his Spirit. Studying his word and following the Spirit will bring God's purpose to light. A person's obedience to the purpose of God produces the fruit of righteousness for his kingdom. The purposes of God can only be understood with the Spirit's help (1 Corinthians 2:14). Discovering God's purpose is important for bringing forth the kingdom of God.

Destiny involves embracing and accomplishing God's purpose. While purpose relates to God's plan for a person, destiny relates to a person's response to God's purpose. All believers are destined to be conformed to the image of Jesus Christ (Romans 8:29). In addition to this general aspect of destiny, there are specific aspects of destiny related to each individual. Destiny does the will of the Father, accomplishing his purpose. The specific destiny for believers involves doing those things they hear and see the Father say and do (John 5:19-20). Fulfilling destiny is the way believers produce fruit for the kingdom of God.

Personal Story about Love

As a young married couple, Sherry and I started ministering to children in low-income areas. We went places to minister where others did not go. Later, we ministered to the homeless, drug addicts, alcoholics, prostitutes, and prisoners. We sincerely loved all people. Before we started ministering we loved those who looked like us and believed like us, which is a limited form of love. After we began ministering to all people, the Spirit produced a supernatural love in our hearts. It was not a love that can be learned from books. This supernatural love grew out of a relationship with the Spirit as we pursued our calling. The love of God which loves all people abides within us.

The Challenge

Share an abundance of spiritual fruit wherever the Spirit leads you.

Producing fruit is not the final goal. The kingdom is the goal for all believers. The kingdom is brought forth by those who do God's will, following the Spirit who produces the fruit. Have a close relationship with the Spirit who will produce fruit through you. As you interact with people, let them partake of the fruit that the Spirit produces through you. Show love, joy, righteousness and other spiritual fruit each and every day. As you continually share spiritual fruit, your fruit will grow, remain, and keep producing.

How does your spiritual fruit help accomplish what is really important in life?

Chapter 6
ANOINTING OF THE SPIRIT

D o you stand in awe of Christ, the Anointed One, living on the inside of you? Multitudes have been amazed at who he is and what he does. The people who believe in Jesus will be amazed and marvel at him (2 Thessalonians 1:10). The anointing is available to all, but it passes over the wise and strong who labor for it. Those who come to the Lord with child-like faith will be filled with his anointing. Like an adventurous child searches a secret garden, those with child-like faith and a sense of awe will be captivated by the anointing within them. The awe of who he is and what he can do is good ground for a person to grow in wisdom.

The anointing is the life of God flowing through believers. At the core of each believer is the mystery of the Spirit's anointing which expresses the depths of the Father and his love for his children. This mystery is the indwelling of the Anointed in you (Colossians 1:27 VOICE)! As believers understand the mystery of the anointing, they know more about themselves and how to live the abundant life Jesus came to give them. In this chapter, you will learn how to increase the influence of the Spirit's anointing in your life.

Introducing the Anointing

The Spirit's anointing is given for ministry to the people. The anointing abides on God's word within believers and flows like rivers out from his throne. The anointing is God's power energized or activated in believers. The inward witness of the anointing confirms the truth. Without the anointing, God's people would doubt the truth but believe lies. Speaking the anointed word destroys the works of the devil and sets people free.

The best way to understand the anointing is to consider the anointing of the Son of God. He was born of the Spirit (Luke 1:35). Men knew him as Jesus, but the Father revealed him as the Christ, the Anointed One (Matthew 16:16-17). Even though he was born the Son of God, he did not teach God's kingdom, heal the sick or perform miracles until he was anointed by the Spirit. After Jesus was baptized in water, the Spirit descended upon him, anointing him with the power of God. At that time, he was immersed in the Spirit and filled with the Spirit (Luke 4:1). Anointed with the Spirit, Jesus was empowered to proclaim profound truths and perform mighty deeds. The Spirit anointed Jesus to proclaim the good news and to set the oppressed free (Luke 4:18-19).

When people receive Jesus as Savior, the Spirit comes with power to live within them. Then when they are filled with the Spirit, God's power is magnified in them. The anointing carries the secrets of God and operates in the supernatural realm. The anointing is here to lead and guide believers to the heart of God. The Spirit's anointing is being poured out everywhere. God is offering his Spirit to everyone (Acts 2:17). Receive the anointing and follow it to glorify God.

Seven Wonders of the Anointing

The anointing is manifest in several wondrous ways. It is poured out to cover, protect and empower believers. It takes away all burdens. Seven of the most important reasons to be anointed with the Spirit are examined below.

1. Awareness of Mysteries

Knowledge and wisdom spring forth out of reverential fear and awe. Worshiping the Lord and regarding him as truly awesome is the beginning of knowledge (Proverbs 1:7). Those who marvel at the Lord and his wisdom have the heart to receive his guidance which comes through the anointing.

The anointing brings an awareness of things hidden from natural senses. It's only by the anointing that believers know the will of God. The anointing abides in willing vessels to bring forth the truth. You have an anointing in you that teaches you the truth (1 John 2:20, 27).

Only by the anointing can people know they are following the Spirit. In making decisions, the most important thing for believers to consider is the anointing within. By the anointing, they can know whether to move forward with an idea, move cautiously or stop. The anointing can help believers in everything they do. It is critical in making decisions like choosing a spouse, planning a career and fulfilling destiny. Professionally, I hired many people and wanted to make the best decision for each position. I gathered the best information available and sought advice from others, but I relied heavily on the anointing within to make the best decisions I could.

2. Strength to Stand

Believers are anointed with the supernatural force of joy. Joy is a mighty force which enables them to stand in adversity. Those who are filled with awe at the wonders of God will break forth in songs of joy (Psalm 65:8). Like kings were anointed at their coronation, Jesus was anointed with joy. "Your God has anointed you, pouring out the oil of joy on you more than on anyone else" (Hebrews 1:9 NLT). His anointing of joy produced a sweet fragrance which attracted people to him. It is called the fragrance of the Anointed One (2 Corinthians 2:15). The anointing brings joy and the strength of the Lord. "The joy of the Lord is your strength" (Nehemiah 8:10). Joy enabled Jesus to endure great suffering on the cross. Just as Jesus was anointed with joy, believers are anointed with his joy. Jesus said, "These things I have spoken to you so that my joy may be in you" (John 15:11).

Believers can rejoice in the midst of trouble knowing they have the victory in Jesus. Paul overflowed with joy in all his great afflictions (2 Corinthians 7:4). As long as believers do not lose their joy, they are stronger than any enemy. When the enemy attacks my body with sickness or pain, I laugh to remind him he is defeated.

3. Power to Move

Jesus was resurrected from the dead by the power of God, and he gave this same power to believers through the Spirit. We have this treasure in jars of clay to show that this all-surpassing power is from God and not from us (2 Corinthians 4:7 NIV). This is the power to boldly act and overcome.

Supernatural power equips believers to do the work of the kingdom. The disciples did not advance the kingdom until they were given power from heaven (Luke 24:49). "You will receive power when the Holy Spirit has come upon you" (Acts 1:8). As the Spirit abides in believers, he empowers them to move into the supernatural realm and do exploits. When empowered, they become transformers of God's power, releasing supernatural power into the natural realm. This power is released by faith to heal the sick, raise the dead and cast out demons. Speaking the word of God and praying can cause an explosion of power.

4. Service to Others

True service comes out of a sense of wonder. When you marvel at who God really is, you humble yourself to serve him and are able to serve others. "Let us show gratitude, by which we may offer to God an acceptable service with reverence and awe" (Hebrews 12:28).

The anointing buries the flesh, preparing believers for service. A woman took an alabaster jar of very expensive perfume and anointed Jesus for burial while he was still alive as a testimony for all believers (John 12:1-7). The fleshly nature contains such things as pride, anger, and unforgiveness. Nothing good dwells in the flesh (Romans 7:18). Our old sinful life died with Christ on the cross so that we would not be slaves to sin (Romans 6:6). "Now those who belong to Christ Jesus have crucified the flesh with its passions and desires" (Galatians 5:24). Even though the flesh has been crucified, it sometimes reappears. For example, when believers are angry or fearful, they let the flesh rise up and control the situation. The anointing will bury the flesh forever.

5. Healing and Deliverance

Believers have access to a powerful healing anointing which flows like a river from the throne of God to bring healing wherever it goes. Fearing the Lord with reverent awe and obedience will heal your body (Proverbs 3:7-8). "Where the river flows everything will live" (Ezekiel 47:9 NIV). That river is the anointing. The Spirit can flow like a mighty river through the hearts of believers (John 7:37). The healing river flows out of the heart of believers and touches those who are hurting, sick and helpless. The anointing heals the sick and sets the captives free.

The anointing can be stored and then released as needed. When anointed handkerchiefs were laid on sick people, the diseases left and the evil spirits departed (Acts 19:11-12). In our ministry, we have seen people in many nations healed and delivered through the use of anointed handkerchiefs. Cancer and brain tumors have disappeared. Other diseases have been burned up.

6. Establishing the Kingdom

It's easy for people to connect with a local congregation which has pastors, staff members, programs, and buildings. They may think that is all people have to do in order to serve God. Natural people can naturally marvel at outstanding preaching, programs, and buildings, but miss the wonders of the kingdom. The kingdom of God is much bigger than any and all local congregations. It is invisible and eternal and supersedes all other kingdoms. A person has to be in awe of God to see the invisible, eternal kingdom. You will not go further in the kingdom than your sense of wonder will carry you.

The anointing establishes the kingdom of God in the lives of believers. The kingdom opens up a world of wonders (Matthew 6:33). It takes the power of God to establish believers in the kingdom of God (Romans 16:25). The anointing helps believers know who they are and where they are going in order to be established in the kingdom.

The anointing makes the kingdom unshakable in the lives of believers. As believers truly experience the kingdom, these experiences cannot be taken from them. While employed in one position, Sherry had seven co-workers who were trained and determined to attack her faith at every level. They were not able to shake her faith because she had truly experienced salvation and entered God's kingdom.

7. Reproducing Life

There is no greater wonder than the wonder of life itself. The breath of God imparted life to the first man, and the breath of Jesus imparted new life to the disciples. The first man Adam became a living being; the last Adam, a life-giving spirit (1 Corinthians 15:45 NIV). Life is supernatural. The Spirit is the one who gives life (John 6:63).

The Lord walked and talked with Adam and Eve in the cool of the evening. He commanded them to be fruitful and multiply (Genesis 1:28). He revealed himself to them so they might reproduce him. Instead, Adam and Eve ate the fruit of the forbidden tree and reproduced themselves. A natural man reproduces himself, a religious man reproduces religion, but the anointing reproduces the anointing. The anointing is given for believers to reproduce spiritual life in the image of the Father.

Bringing forth life is part of the reproduction anointing. Believers are anointed to propagate the anointing. Propagate means to be fruitful and to multiply. Believers propagate the anointing by leading people to Jesus, instructing them on the anointing and laying hands on them to be filled with the Spirit. The anointing is at the heart of making disciples.

Increasing the Anointing

There is a cost to the anointing. As shown in the parable of the ten virgins, there is a price to be paid for the precious oil (Matthew 25:1-9). Oil in the parable symbolizes the anointing. The virgins who wanted more oil to fuel their light were instructed to go where oil was bought and sold. Like all other precious things, there are sacrifices made to gain the anointing. The greater the sacrifices made for the anointing, the greater the anointing a believer carries. For more anointing, believers pay the price of sacrificing their will to do the Father's will. Jesus said, "If anyone wishes to come after me, he must deny himself, and take up his cross and follow me" (Matthew 16:24). The anointing costs everything.

The greatest sacrifice for the anointing is shown in the life of Jesus. As the second person in the Godhead, Jesus has always been God. "In the beginning was the word, and the word was with God, and the word was God" (John 1:1). Throughout eternity, he was filled with glory and majesty, but he gave all of it up to take on flesh and become a sacrificial lamb for all mankind. What a great price he paid. The Father anointed him with the Holy Spirit and power.

Personal relationships with the Father, his Son, and his Spirit are critical for receiving more anointing. These three members of the Godhead have unique roles concerning the anointing. The Father anoints believers with his Spirit. The Son is the Christ, the Anointed One, within believers. Christ in you is the hope of glory (Colossians 1:27). Since each member of the Godhead has a unique role in the anointing, believers who try to limit any member of the Godhead are just limiting the anointing in their own lives.

The anointing is on the revealed word of God, so believers become more anointed by hearing the anointed word and studying the word under the guidance of the Spirit. When they are filled with the revealed word, they can draw on the anointing within for every situation.

A believer's anointing can be increased by developing strong relationships with anointed believers. "He who walks with wise men will be wise" (Proverbs 13:20). believers can impart the anointing to others. Pursuing relationships ordained by God can have a great impact on a believer's anointing.

Personal Story on the Anointing

When Sherry and I were filled with the Spirit, we knew we had to go where people believed in the works of the Spirit. Some people advised us to go to Bible school or seminary, but the anointing within led us to a small, rural fellowship 40 miles from our home. Its pastor was a gifted teacher who operated in all the gifts of the Spirit. His ministry was widely known for healing and miracles. People would come there from nearby and far away, seeking to be healed. Many would stay only until they were healed, but some stayed and became a part of the ministry. We were actively involved in the ministry there. We learned a great deal about the word of God from his teaching and received an anointing for healing and miracles.

It cost us a lot to be built up in the word of God and to receive an anointing for healing and miracles. We traveled to the fellowship three times a week for eleven years. In total, we drove more than 100 thousand miles to be taught the word of God. Our children did their homework for school in the car on the way to services and slept in the car on the way home. The travel involved a sacrifice for all of us. We passed by a lot of fellowships which were more conveniently located than the one we were attending, but we wanted the power of God operating in our lives rather than a form of godliness.

The Challenge

Diligently seek the fresh revelation of Christ, the Anointed One.

ENLIGHTENED AND EMPOWERED

There is more of God's word to be revealed by the Spirit than you know. Never become complacent with what you know and what you experienced with the Lord. Study the word under the guidance of the Spirit. Marvel at the anointing within you. Let the anointing lead you and strengthen you. Desire the Spirit's fresh anointing oil!

How do you guard against complacency and elitism?

Chapter 7
SPIRITUAL MATURITY

Believers are heirs of all things but control nothing until they mature spiritually. "As long as the heir is a child, he does not differ at all from a slave although he is the owner of everything" (Galatians 4:1). It's time to press forward toward maturity. "Let us move beyond the elementary teachings about Christ and be taken forward to maturity" (Hebrews 6:1 NIV). Many different spiritual factors contribute to the process of maturity, including love, faith, and grace. However, these factors are only part of a bigger process which involves spiritual relationships. In this chapter, you will learn what spiritual maturity means and how you can mature. The focus is placed on relationships with the Spirit and spiritual fathers which are crucial to spiritual maturity.

Introducing Spiritual Maturity

Spiritual maturity is the ongoing process of becoming more like Jesus Christ. It involves the development of strong character traits which reflect God's divine nature. God promised his children could share in his nature to become like

59

him (2 Peter 1:4). Believers begin to reflect his nature as they mature or grow up spiritually by learning about God and building a relationship with him. Any two can walk together only when they agree (Amos 3:3). Speaking what God says and doing what he does is an outward expression of his character within a person. As believers mature spiritually, they become more sensitive to the Spirit and less sensitive to fleshly desires (Romans 8:5-6). Then the things above become more real, and the desires for the things on the earth diminish.

Enoch walked closely with God and was translated to be with him through faith (Hebrews 11:5). As he walked with God, he matured to be more like him and to please him. He had such a strong relationship with God that he desired eternal things more than earthly pleasures. God took him into the supernatural realm, and he was no longer in this realm. As believers draw close to God, he gives them his desires and abilities, and they begin to change the way they think and act. He imparts his faith, his love, and his peace. Believers can merge into him as they abide in him and he abides in them. "If you abide in me, and my words abide in you, ask whatever you wish, and it will be done for you" (John 15:7).

The character of a person is critical in his/her journey to mature spiritually. A person is known by his/her character. For a believer, love should be the most prominent characteristic of his/her life and the deciding factor in every situation (2

Corinthians 5:14). Love never stops and never fails (1 Corinthians 13:8, 13).

Sonship

The heavenly Father demonstrates his great love by adopting sons into his family. All those who believe and accept Jesus as Savior become sons in the family of God (John 1:12 J. B. Phillips Translation, PHILLIPS). This verse refers to immature sons. "Gone is the distinction between . . . male and female (Galatians 3:28 PHILLIPS). All those who have faith in Christ are already sons of God, so both men and women can be called sons of God.

When sons are first adopted into the family of God, they are immature spiritual infants. Spiritual infants are self-centered, still working out issues of their own identity and life-purpose. "Brethren, do not be children in your thinking; yet in evil be infants, but in your thinking, be mature" (1 Corinthians 14:20). Spiritual infants are expected to mature over time, but the process of maturing spiritually is not a natural process. "By this time, you ought to be teachers yourselves, yet here I find you need someone to sit down with you and go over the basics on God again" (Hebrews 5:12 MSG). Spiritual intervention is needed to mature God's sons.

Knowing the Father's love is what allows a believer to become a son. The Father nurtures and cares for his children. He gives them instruction and training through the Spirit

(Ephesians 6:14). He also disciplines those sons whom he loves (Hebrews 12:7-8). This discipline is not through accidents, sickness or natural things, but he uses the Spirit to guide and convict the hearts of those sons. The Spirit changes the thinking of a son and causes his/her mind to be renewed to the word of God. (1 Corinthians 2:16) This discipline is needed for maturity.

Maturing by the Spirit's Light and Power

All spiritual transformation is by the light and power of the Spirit. When the earth was void and without form, the Spirit transformed it. He brought light into the darkness and made earth inhabitable for God's creation. Similarly, the Spirit transforms and matures sons with his light and power.

The Spirit brings sons out of being self-centered and helps them see spiritual things and be concerned about others. Under his guidance, they no longer walk in darkness but clearly see the purposes of the Father. As sons hear and recognize the voice of the Spirit, they become more sensitive to spiritual things. Their sensitivity to spiritual things is a sign of maturity. "For all who are being led by the Spirit of God, these are sons of God" (Romans 8:14). Only mature sons consistently follow the guidance of the Spirit.

Maturing by the Guidance and Impartation of Spiritual Fathers

Many ministers teach and preach God's word without maturing his sons. It takes spiritual fathers to equip and mature God's sons to bring forth Christ in them. There are only a few spiritual fathers among the multitudes of ministers teaching and preaching God's word (1 Corinthians 4:14-15). God connects spiritual fathers with their sons to mature them.

Many times, old foundations of doctrines and traditions of men must be destroyed before believers can mature in the Lord. Also, wrong thinking must be replaced with God's word. The bedrock of a person's thoughts must come in line with the truth. Spiritual fathers lay a foundation of spiritual principles in their sons so they will be able to bring forth the Christ in their lives. They draw potential out of their sons by helping them discover their purpose and equipping them to fulfill it. As a spiritual father, Paul labored in prayer for those he called his sons so that they would mature. He desired that Christ would be manifested in their lives (Galatians 4:19). Paul's message to spiritual infants was not with wise and persuasive words but with a demonstration of the Spirit's power (1 Corinthians 2:4, 3:1-2). Mere words would not mature them, but the Spirit's power would.

Spiritual fathers teach their sons to pray and be led by the Spirit. Then the sons will know that membership in a religious organization does not substitute for a personal relationship with the heavenly Father, his Son, and his Spirit. A spiritual father's message is passed on from one generation to the next. Paul wrote to his son Timothy to keep passing on the same message. "The things you have heard me say in the presence of many witnesses entrust to reliable people who will also be qualified to teach others" (2 Timothy 2:2 NIV).

The love of a father sets a son on a path of life to be successful. The son may choose to leave this path, but the love of the father will draw him back. When the prodigal son came to his senses, he returned to his father who loved him (Luke 15:17-20).

Fathers can make a big difference in the lives of their children. Sherry and I observed some startling patterns among the people we ministered to in different venues. The homeless people who came to our mission had little interaction with their fathers. Less than 10% of these homeless people were positively influenced by their fathers. Those people who were incarcerated in jails and prisons had a little more interaction with their fathers. About 25% of them were positively influenced by their fathers. The people whom we would consider to be successful in life, as measured by their incomes, careers, and marriages, had the greatest interaction with their fathers. More than 90% of these people were positively influenced by their fathers.

Conformed to the Image of Christ

It is important to remember the goal of a spiritual son is to be like Christ. As long as they keep this goal as their focus, they will stay on the right path. Being Christ-like is not based on performance. Instead, sons are to let the Christ within them dominate their lives and manifest himself through them. As sons begin to talk like Christ and do what he does, they can share his glory (Colossians 1:27). Like Paul, every mature son can proclaim that it is no longer I that lives, but it is Christ that lives in me (Galatians 2:20).

Personal Story about Spiritual Maturity

As Sherry and I began to seek the Lord, we were both filled with the Spirit's light and power. The Spirit began to open up God's word to us. In the religious system, no one wanted to train us up and release us into our purpose. They wanted to use us to their own advantage. The Spirit showed us that we needed a spiritual father to encourage and help us.

We prayed and asked the Lord to send us a spiritual father. Then we were introduced to an apostle who was willing to work with us. He showed us how Paul and Barnabas were set apart to do God's work (Acts 13:1-5). Then he said it was time for us to be set apart so we could do the work we were called to do. The Lord joined our hearts together, and he became our spiritual father. We began to mature spiritually as we went to be with him and he came to be with us. He also sent several ministers to help us. Later, he asked several apostles and prophets to lay hands on us and to send us forth to do the work we were called to do. There was a shift in the heavens that day, and doors began to open up for us. Since then, we have been ministering with authority and power in many nations.

The Challenge

Mature in your walk with the Lord by staying focused on Christ.

Diligently pursue God and his ways over your lifetime, and you will discover his nature and character traits are growing inside of you. Persevere through the difficult situations in your life and the merits of your character will be proven. Be sensitive to the Spirit and joined with a spiritual father who watches for your soul so you can mature spiritually. Spiritual maturity is not the final goal, but it is a necessary element for fulfilling the destiny to which you were called. As you mature spiritually, you will walk with more authority and power.

How do you demonstrate that God's light and power are at work in your life?

Chapter 8
STRATEGIC GRACE RELATIONSHIPS

Touching life together through personal relationships is the heart of God's kingdom. He joins or connects people together in relationship with him and with each other as it pleases him. "God has placed the members, each one of them, in the body, just as he desired" (1 Corinthians 12:18). He draws people to himself and connects people together by his Spirit. Men want to limit relationships by doctrine, denominations and local congregations, but there are no such limitations in the spirit. Both divine connections and divine assignments are used in fulfilling God's purpose for building personal relationships. Friends, mentors and spiritual fathers matter more the higher a person wants to climb. In this chapter, you will learn how to build God's kingdom on ordained relationships by grace. It examines how to build and sustain meaningful relationships with grace.

Introducing Strategic Grace Relationships

In God's kingdom, people are supernaturally joined together through ordained relationships by grace. We call these ordained relationships grace joints because they are built and sustained by God's grace. The body of Christ is joined together through the support and contributions of every joint (Ephesians 4:16). The body grows as the joints supply grace to one another. These joints are believers whom God supernaturally connects. When each joint works properly, God increases the body of Christ in love. Grace joints are important in the kingdom because growth only occurs in the joints: Christ uses joints and ligaments to hold his body together, as God causes it to grow (Colossians 2:19). God's growth is only with grace joints, so any growth plan which does not focus on joints or ordained relationships is ineffective.

The relationship between Jonathan and David is one of the best known and most powerful personal relationships described in the word of God. Jonathan was the crown prince and next in line to be king of Israel, but the Lord had anointed David to be king. It appeared Jonathan and David would be on different sides in a power struggle, but God joined their hearts together after Jonathan heard David speak about his faith and trust in God (1 Samuel 18:1-3). Jonathan stripped himself of his robe and armor and gave them to David (1 Samuel 18:4). This gesture showed Jonathan greatly honored and respected David, and now we understand it symbolized his right to ascend the throne was being transferred to David.

By walking in the world and spending time with the lost, believers can touch them with God's love and grace. As their hearts are opened, the possibility of sharing the word of God with them will increase. The opportunity to share God's love will flow effectively out of personal relationships. Many will respond to his love expressed through personal relationships and be saved. While Philip was in the midst of a great revival, God gave him a new assignment to reach one lost person. An angel told Philip to go south on the desert road between Jerusalem and Gaza (Acts 8:26). As instructed he went down to the desert and saw a man from Ethiopia traveling in a chariot. The Spirit said, "Go up and join this chariot" (Acts 8:29). Philip ran up to the chariot and was able to share the gospel with the man and then baptize him in water.

God assigns you to build personal relationships with some people but not all those with whom you come in contact. You are responsible only for "those who are allotted to your charge" (1 Peter 5:3). It is very important to seek the Lord to determine whom God is assigning to you. Spiritual growth occurs with your unique allotment, not with the masses of people.

Five Keys for Growing Together in Grace

Other than a person's relationship with God, the most important thing in life is mature, fulfilling personal relationships for that is where God promises his blessings. His blessings are poured out on his people who unite for a purpose (Psalm 133:1-3). He ordains personal relationships and gives believers the grace to operate in these relationships. When each party freely contributes grace to others in the relationship, all the parties benefit from the relationship. Operating in grace means that a person is led by the Spirit of grace, is strengthened by grace and contributes grace to others. Grace relationships or joints are supernatural relationships which make them stronger than natural ones. Even when difficulties arise in a grace relationship, the parties will not abandon the relationship but allow the Spirit of grace to reconcile them.

In God and by his grace, relationships become strong and meaningful. People need to walk together in relationships to discover their God-given purpose and fulfill destiny. Those who are pursuing purpose and destiny are on a journey of discovery and personal growth. Adventure, risk, and satisfaction from fulfillment are encountered on the journey. All of those on the journey are called and equipped by God, but also have to be accompanied by others who have answered the call. They help each other with wise counsel and encouragement. Those who are further along on the journey can offer a helping hand to those who follow. Supportive relationships are needed for people to advance in their journey. "May you all continue the journey with your spirits strengthened by the grace of the Lord Jesus, the Anointed One" (Philippians 4:23 VOICE). Relationships with those on the journey help provide success and safety.

The word of God is filled with examples of great leaders who intentionally developed relationships with people to help them fulfill purpose and destiny. David was a shepherd before Samuel anointed him to be king, and Elisha was a farmer before Elijah called him. Peter, James, and John were fishermen before Jesus called them, and they wanted to return to fishing after his death and resurrection. Jesus had to follow up with them after his resurrection in order for them to fulfill their purpose and destiny as apostles. Paul described himself as a father to Timothy and Titus, as well as others. He built lasting relationships with them and continued to communicate with them when he was not able to be with them. Paul recognized the role of grace in building relationships. "By the grace of God, I am what I am, and his grace toward me did not prove vain; but I labored even more than all of them, yet not I, but the grace of God with me" (1 Corinthians 15:10). This section will help you understand how to have relationships God's way.

1. Grace Reconciles Relationships

The reconciling force of grace is a fundamental force in building a strong relationship. Through the free gift of grace by Jesus Christ, many are reconciled to God and made right with him (2 Corinthians 5:18; Ephesians 2:8-9). They can stand confidently in this relationship of grace, knowing that God is their Father and that he has glorious things for them. The heavenly realm becomes open and accessible to them. Believers are instructed to seek those things which are above

(Colossians 3:1-2). They have access to the throne of grace where they can obtain grace, as well as mercy and help (Hebrews 4:16). Thus, believers can obtain more grace by spending time at the throne of grace in the presence of the Lord.

Evil desires can damage relationships, but the things of this world become less important than eternal things when believers spend time in the Lord's presence. As believers experience the heavenly realm, they walk in great power. Operating in God's grace is evidence that a person has experienced the heavenly realm.

2. Grace Invites the Presence of the Spirit

It is possible to welcome and receive the Spirit of grace and then see him move into a situation. It is also possible to grieve the Spirit of grace and see him depart from a situation. When the Spirit has removed himself from a situation, the believer has two options, either to continue operating only with natural abilities or to follow the leading of the Spirit and leave. Continuing to operate only with natural abilities will make the situation worse, but following the Spirit will lead to peace and victory.

The Spirit of grace abides where there is peace, love, harmony, and faith. Relationships flourish in this positive environment. On the other hand, fighting and arguing push the Spirit away. There is little or no grace to help strengthen relationships in such a negative environment. Maintain a positive, faith-filled environment in personal relationships for them to grow.

3. Grace Strengthens Believers

Believers will find that their natural abilities are inadequate to build strong relationships. Even when believers are weak, God's grace is powerful. His grace is sufficient for power is perfected in weakness (2 Corinthians 12:9). As long as believers function where they have grace, they will be able to build strong relationships, stand against attacks of the enemy and walk in victory. Use the grace you receive to strengthen others.

When pressures on personal relationships are the greatest, many temptations abound. In such cases, believers need strengthening to withstand temptations. Grace strengthens believers to pursue ways of escape rather than yielding to temptations.

4. Grace Serves Others

Use grace in a way that will best serve others (1 Peter 4:10). You can serve others through gracious words and gracious actions by speaking and acting on the word of God. The words of a wise man are gracious (Ecclesiastes 10:12). When believers operate in grace, they will know how to answer for the hope that is within them. They do not need to plan what to say. The Spirit will fill their mouth with the words of the Father (Matthew 10:18-20). Knowing what the Father would have a believer say in a particular situation is an operation of grace. The word of God is full of grace and truth, and it is called the word of grace (John 1:14; Acts 14:3, 20:32).

God's grace supernaturally empowers and energizes believers to live a victorious life. As long as believers function in the area where they have grace, they will be successful. However, believers cannot effectively minister grace to others until they have received grace and operated in it.

5. Grace Fashions the Future

The eyes of faith see the future, but it takes grace to build it. For all future time, God will show the riches of his grace by being kind to us in Christ Jesus (Ephesians 2:7). When people look at current situations through natural eyes, they may see obstacles and impossibilities; but when they are strengthened by grace, they can see the possibilities. Look beyond present circumstances and begin to fashion the future for yourself and others by relying on grace to supernaturally overcome natural situations and change circumstances.

Personal Story on Grace Joints

Sherry and I learned about grace joints while we were teaching the word of God and ministering to people in a low-income community. Many people were coming to our services, and the small building which we were using could not hold them. We rented a larger building a few blocks away, thinking many of these same people would go with us. However, the Spirit said we were not joined with any of those people, so we could not build with them. God's people can build only on joints in the body of Christ. I argued with the Spirit because we had led those people to the Lord and taught them the word of God. But I was wrong, and the Spirit was right. None of those people went with us to the larger building even though it was within walking distance from the small building. Our ministry grew but not with those people, because the Lord had not joined them with us. He had other joints for them, and they had to follow the Spirit to find their own joints. It takes the Spirit to reveal the ordained joints where spiritual building can occur.

When Sherry and I began our ministry years ago, we began building programs like we had seen others build them. This was the fourth plateau on which we were trapped. The people with whom we were joined started coming to be with us and observing our progress. They told us that we were building incorrectly. They said we were building on a religious skeleton which needed to be destroyed. We did not know any other way to build than what we had observed with others. We had to follow the Spirit to build the way God wanted us to build. We are pioneers with a unique ministry fashioned by the Spirit.

Sherry and I pursue personal relationships with many of those people whom God places in our paths, while they are yet imperfect. We realize once they are perfected and have everything together they will have no need for us. We pursue relationships with those who may not be in a position to benefit us. In the beginning, friendship is the primary reason to pursue a relationship. However, many of our relationships mature into other areas. For example, some people ask us to provide oversight in their lives and hold them accountable.

We are always seeking the Lord to find out who he has joined with us. When people come to us and ask to join themselves with us, we try to help them while we are seeking the Lord for direction. The Spirit soon reveals whether he has joined them with us. Sometimes people claim to be joined with us when the Spirit says they are not. Our efforts with those whom God has not joined with us are not as fruitful as our efforts with those who have been joined with us. The Spirit often assigns us to work with people before they really understand anything about grace relationships. We work with them while we can and hope our relationship will grow.

The Challenge

Nurture your relationships that are ordained by God.
A few relationships ordained by God are more important than thousands made by man. Wasting your time on meaningless engagements may make you popular, but investing your time and effort wisely in strategic relationships ordained by God makes you powerful. Your spiritual growth occurs only in the relationships God ordained for you. Ask the Spirit about your

STRATEGIC GRACE RELATIONSHIPS

ordained relationships and invest your time and effort in those.
Be cautious about who you give access to your life and with
whom you partner. Make friends with people who will push
you to make changes in life that matter in the end. Build
genuine connections based on friendship, trust, and care.

How do relationships help you manifest the reality of
Christ?

Chapter 9
GIFTS OF THE SPIRIT

Passionately desire and cultivate the gifts which come from the Spirit. "Follow the way of love and eagerly desire gifts of the Spirit, especially prophecy" (1 Corinthians 14:1 NIV). God wants his people to be informed about the gifts and to know how to flow with the Spirit in using them. All the gifts come from the same Spirit to strengthen, encourage and comfort people. In this chapter, you will learn how to identify and operate the nine gifts of the Spirit.

Some people are weak and sick in their bodies and minds and need to hear from God. The gifts of the Spirit can be used to help them. When the Spirit comes into a person's life, he brings the fruit and the gifts of the Spirit. The gifts operate only through the fruit. Without love, you are nothing and what you say has no impact (1 Corinthians 13:1-8). One must have faith to operate in the gifts. When Jesus ascended to the Father, he sent the Spirit to be with us. Spiritual gifts are part of the Spirit's responsibility. In the Old Testament, only the prophets and seers prophesied what they heard and saw. Under the new covenant, every believer can operate the gifts and give them to others. The gifts operate through believers for them to be given away. "Freely you received, freely give" (Matthew 10:8).

Introducing Gifts of the Spirit

The gifts of the Spirit flow out of the love of God. They point people to God and show forth his glory and his majesty. All gifts operate by the Spirit (1 Corinthians 12:11). Opportunities for believers to help others with these gifts may exist in any place. Wherever believers are loving people, they can operate in the gifts. God is looking for willing vessels through which his gifts can operate.

Through the gifts of the Spirit, believers hear and see what God is doing in the spirit and what he wants to do in the natural realm. Jesus provided the pattern for operating in spiritual gifts. He spoke only what he heard the Father say, and he did only what he saw the Father do (John 5:19, 8:26). Spiritual gifts are special endowments related to wisdom, knowledge, great faith, healing, miracles, prophecy, discerning of spirits, unknown languages, and interpretation of unknown languages (1 Corinthians 12:8-10). These gifts can be grouped into three broad categories: inspirational gifts, verbal gifts, and power gifts. These gifts are discussed below.

Inspirational Gifts

The inspirational gifts motivate people to believe God and act on what they believe. These gifts are the words of knowledge and wisdom and discerning of spirits. The word of knowledge makes a fact known which was not known in the natural. For example, a word of knowledge may point out a person with a particular ailment. The Spirit makes this fact known to correct the ailment. The word of wisdom gives supernatural direction to a person or group. In general, wisdom gives understanding on how to use knowledge. Discerning of spirits can see angelic beings and evil spirits. This gift often operates before a believer casts out an evil spirit.

On a consistent basis, the gift of discerning of spirits is in operation in Sherry's life. She has seen both angels and demonic forces. Some of the angels she saw have been those who are sent to carry people from this world to the next. They are all tall and without wings. They stand ready in hospital rooms or bedrooms. She has also seen warring angels, those with swords ready to war against the forces of evil. The demonic forces she has seen have appeared like snakes, lizards and other creatures. They have been primarily green. Some have had huge teeth. The Spirit always shows her what to do and what to say to these evil forces to take authority over them.

Verbal Gifts

The verbal gifts speak what was heard in the supernatural realm to encourage and comfort people. These gifts are the abilities to speak in unknown languages, interpret these unknown languages, and prophecy. Speaking in unknown languages is a public utterance of a heavenly language which has to be interpreted for the people to understand. Interpreting unknown languages provides understanding to what was said in the heavenly languages. In contrast to these gifts, the believer's prayer language is generally considered as a private prayer language used to build up his/her own faith. "But you, beloved, building yourselves up on your most holy faith, praying in the Holy Spirit" (Jude 1:20). Any believer who is filled with the Spirit can pray in the spirit without having to interpret the message.

The gift of prophecy is equivalent to speaking in unknown languages and interpreting these languages because prophecy can be understood by the people. The one who prophesies speaks to people for their strengthening, encouraging and comfort (1 Corinthians 14:3 NIV). It builds up faith in the people. Years ago, I gave a prophecy about new territories that the Lord wanted his people to discover. The provisions of his unexplored territories are available to those who diligently seek them. His provisions can never be exhausted, but the things he shows believers belong to them. This message continues to resonate in my soul, propelling me to move forward in the Lord.

Power Gifts

The power gifts do what was seen in the supernatural realm. These gifts are great faith, healing, and miracles. The measure of faith which is given to every believer might be considered as the common faith in contrast to the spiritual gift of faith. "God has allotted to each a measure of faith" (Romans 12:3). The gift of faith is a powerful force which magnifies a believer's common faith. The gift of faith is used for others when their faith is weak or they cannot activate their own faith.

The gift of healings is given to heal the sick. It is an expression of God's love for his people, and those who operate the gift of healings are compassionate for those who are sick. Like Jesus, they are moved by compassion and pray frequently for the sick. While believers can have faith to be healed and faith to pray for others to be healed, the gift of healings releases tremendous healing power beyond what an individual already believes.

The gift of miracles is the unlimited miraculous power which can change natural situations. Miracles happen when God supernaturally intervenes. When Sherry was teaching God's word one evening, she saw a man there that had an arm cut off below the elbow. He sold vegetables and fruits from a tiny cart every day on a busy intersection to earn a living. As she began to minister to the people, she saw this man's arm grow in the spirit realm. Compassion rose up in Sherry, and she asked Jesus to stretch out his arm. The arm of the man began to grow miraculously, and he walked out of the building that night with two arms. God is a miracle-working God.

Purposes for the Gifts of the Spirit

Gifts of the Spirit are given to be used for God's glory. Speak the utterances of God and serve others "so that in all things God may be glorified through Jesus Christ" (1 Peter 4:11). They are to be used to help each other. "As each one has received a special gift, employ it in serving one another as good stewards of the manifold grace of God" (1 Peter 4:10). Spiritual gifts are given to each person for the common good or benefit of all people (1 Corinthians 12:7).

Gifts of the Spirit bring the lost into the kingdom of God. People look at the signs and wonders and declare there is a God and they want to be with him (1 Corinthians 14:24-25). Jesus compels believers to go into the highways and byways telling people to come into the kingdom of God, not into a particular congregation or denomination. Those people who are willing to let the spiritual gifts flow through them can be very effective in reaching the lost. One summer day when Sherry was feeding the homeless on the street, a teenage boy came up for a hot dog but got much more. The Spirit rose up inside Sherry, activating the word of knowledge. She was able to tell this teenager how he was beaten with a leather strap by his dad until he ran away from home. Then the Spirit shared the story of how Jesus was beaten and how he loved this teenager. The teenager began to cry and accepted Jesus as savior right there on the street. The Spirit operated the gifts through Sherry to bring him to salvation. God wants the gifts to flow freely in the body. Be a willing vessel fit for the master's use.

Gifts of the Spirit help the saints and build up the body of Christ. Anyone who shares a spiritual gift in a meeting should build up the church (1 Corinthians 14:26). "For you can all prophesy one by one, so that all may learn and all may be exhorted" (1 Corinthians 14:31).

Receiving Gifts of the Spirit

A gift can be offered to someone, but it becomes a blessing only when it is received. Paul wrote that he longed to see the people in Rome so he might impart some spiritual gift unto them (Romans 1:11). Spiritual gifts can be received by a person acting on the word of God alone or allowing others to pray for him/her to receive the gifts. Paul described how spiritual leaders prayed for Timothy and imparted a spiritual gift to him. They prophesied over him and laid hands on him so he could receive the gift. "Do not neglect the spiritual gift within you, which was bestowed on you through prophetic utterance with the laying on of hands by the presbytery" (1 Timothy 4:14). Believers have to be willing vessels for spiritual gifts to operate through them. Natural thoughts about personal inabilities and limitations will hinder the flow of spiritual gifts through a believer. The vessels through which God chooses to deliver his gifts are frail, but the source of these gifts is holy and perfect. Recognizing every good and perfect gift is from above will help believers operate in spiritual gifts.

Activating Gifts of the Spirit

By faith, believers can expect spiritual gifts to operate through them. When the gifts are being activated at first, believers can ask for instructions and help from spiritual leaders, pray for divine guidance and put a demand on the spiritual gifts within them.

We help young people activate and develop spiritual gifts by providing a safe environment in which they can prophesy and pray for people. Small group settings work well for these spiritual efforts. We instruct them about prophecy, give them opportunities to prophesy to one another and give them gentle feedback on their efforts to operate in the supernatural realm. Their initial efforts may seem small, but such efforts can help them gain confidence about hearing from the Spirit and prophesying those things which are worthwhile to others.

Personal Stories about Spiritual Gifts

Sherry and I searched for a place where the gifts of the Spirit would be in operation. We found a congregation where the pastor operated in the gifts, and we were comfortable in that place for a time. There we experienced healings and miracles and saw all of the gifts in operation. However, the pastor was the only one who regularly operated in the gifts. It was wonderful to watch others operate in the light and power of God, but we could never fulfill our destiny by only being observers. This was the fifth plateau on which we were trapped. We had to keep climbing higher up God's mountain by doing what we were called to do.

Several of the gifts operate in my life, including prophecy, tongues, and interpretation of tongues. The most prominent gifts in my life are healings and wisdom. I am passionate about healing, teaching others, and praying for the sick. Wisdom knows the mind and heart of God. I am able to share God's wisdom with many of those whom I encounter. His wisdom delivers people and sets them on a path to fulfill destiny. These gifts help fulfill my calling to disciple, equip and father believers.

Sherry operates in all the gifts, but the power gifts and prophecy are most prominent in her life. Even as a child, Sherry knew things about what had happened to people and what was about to happen. She did not ask to know these things but knew them by the Spirit. At such an early age she did not know what to do with this information. The operation of spiritual gifts has intensified in her life in recent times. The Spirit told her that he would increase her abilities as a warrior prophetess to combat and expel evil and darkness. When the Spirit shows her things, she is quick to respond with prayer and action. Also, in recent times her eyes have become more sensitive to the supernatural realm. At times she can see inside a person's body and know exactly what needs to be corrected. The Lord has healed the sick, performed miracles and raised the dead as Sherry speaks out what she sees and hears from the Lord.

The Challenge

In loving and serving others, distribute the gifts God has given you.

Offer yourself as a vessel through which all the gifts can flow freely. Receive and activate the gifts by faith. The greatest gift is Jesus Christ, so use the other gifts to point people to him. Be sensitive to the Spirit's guidance for everywhere you go someone will need the gifts which operate in you. Take authority over unclean spirits, cast them out, heal the sick, and set the captives free.

Considering that God has given you all things in Christ, what can you give to him?

Chapter 10
STRATEGIC PRAYERS

W hy do people pray? Most people pray for one reason and that is to change things. They want to see changes in people and situations. Many of these prayers are ineffective because the people who pray are led by needs they see and not by the unseen Spirit. Praying by faith rather than by the things you see can be pleasing to the Lord and effective. "We walk by faith, not by sight" (2 Corinthians 5:7). The word of God gives one reason to pray and that is to glorify the Father. Do everything for the glory of God (1 Corinthians 10:31). In this chapter, you will discover how to pray strategically so God will be glorified and your prayers will not fail.

Introducing Strategic Prayers

Strategic prayers are carefully planned to fulfill a divine purpose. Such prayers are built on sound Biblical principles and always effective. This section addresses the prayers of Jesus and Paul and their teachings about prayer. People who are serious about prayer can learn much from their prayers and their instructions on prayer.

How Jesus Prayed

When Jesus prayed, he expressed the will of the Father, and his prayers were always effective. Jesus is the expression of the Father for he is the word of God. "In the beginning was the word and the word was with God" (John 1:1). Jesus knew he could do nothing on his own, so he always prayed about everything he did. "The Son can do nothing by himself; he can do only what he sees his Father doing" (John 5:19 NIV). Even though Jesus was the Son of God, he only did what he saw the Father do.

Jesus always prayed the same way. He first listened to the Father, and then he prayed what he heard the Father say. "The things I speak, I speak just as the Father has told me" (John 12:50). The words Jesus spoke to the world and prayed to the Father were first spoken by the Father. Jesus only prayed those things he heard the Father say.

Jesus saw many sick and crippled people at the pool of Bethesda, but he was not led by their needs (John 5:2-9). In the midst of a multitude of needs, Jesus ministered to only one man. He told the lame man, "Get up, pick up your pallet, and walk" (John 5:8). Immediately, the man became well and recovered strength. Jesus spoke the Father's words, and the man responded to these words and walked away healed.

Jesus did not react to the request by Mary and Martha to heal their sick brother Lazarus as they hoped (John 11:1-15). Instead, Jesus chose to glorify the Father. He said, "This sickness is not to end in death, but for the glory of God" (John 11:4). Jesus was not led by needs, nor did he yield to their pressure. He did the things which would glorify the Father. He never prayed for something until he heard what the Father said. He prayed the perfect will of the Father. Effective prayers express the Father's will, not the believer's will, desires or even needs. Jesus prayed to the Father, "not my will, but yours be done" (Luke 22:42).

How Jesus Taught Others to Pray

Jesus taught about prayer in the Sermon on the Mount, as well as elsewhere (Matthew 5-7). His message contrasted the attitude of the heart with outward appearances. Those who have only an outward form of prayer cannot expect anything from God. He taught about prayers being based on relationships, which make them relational prayers. This type of prayer requires believers to spend time with the Father, seeking his heart and guidance through his Spirit. Only the Spirit knows the deep secrets of the Father's heart (1 Corinthians 2:10). It takes the Spirit to guide believers into the deep things of the Father and develop a vibrant prayer life.

The disciples asked to be taught how to pray, so Jesus gave them the Lord's Prayer (Luke 11:1-4). This prayer helps release the spirit man. When Jesus prayed, he was already communing spirit-to-spirit with the Father, but his disciples were not at the same place in life as Jesus. The Lord's Prayer has all the spiritual elements needed by the spirit man. In general, the spirit desires for the things expressed in the Lord's Prayer. First, the prayer connects the spirit man to his family origins. Since his Father is the holy God of heaven, the spirit man is holy, godly and part of the universal family in heaven and earth. Second, it projects the Father's kingdom upon the earth. There is no difference between his kingdom in heaven and his kingdom on earth. Third, it makes daily provision for the spirit man. Fourth, it establishes forgiveness as the environment in which the spirit man lives and thrives. Fifth, it sets the pathway for the spirit man as righteousness.

The Lord's Prayer activates God's Spirit. Jesus spoke about the outpouring of the Spirit shortly after teaching the Lord's Prayer. He said your heavenly Father will give his Spirit to those who ask him (Luke 11:13). Believers can activate the spirit man in their lives by praying the Lord's Prayer. Also, believers can use the Lord's Prayer to help make a transition from natural thinking to effectively praying in the spirit.

How Paul Prayed

Paul's prayer life was insightful, continuous and led by the Spirit. His prayers were inspired by God's Spirit because all scripture is inspired by the Spirit (2 Peter 1:20-21). Paul was devoted to prayer. He prayed for the people he knew, people he had not yet met, the nation of Israel and all saints. Rather than using his prayers and faith to achieve his own desires, he prayed for the Father's will to be done.

Paul's prayers were effective for the people of his day, and they continue to be effective today. He cast out demons, caused the lame to walk and healed the sick. When Paul and Silas prayed in prison, the doors were opened and the prisoners were set free (Acts 16:25-26). His prayers produced the expected results. Many of Paul's prayers were spiritual and the results were spiritual, so the results are not obvious to natural senses.

Paul prayed for the foundations to be laid in the lives of believers. He prayed their love would abound and they would have a revelation of the knowledge of Jesus Christ. He prayed that believers would fulfill their destiny. These prayers provide excellent guidance for prayer warriors today. They can pray for people to receive a revelation of Jesus Christ and to fulfill their destiny.

Paul was an apostle and he prayed powerful apostolic prayers. He prayed for believers to know the Father, their calling, their inheritance and the power available to them (Ephesians 1:17-20). He prayed their lives would center on Christ and they would know his love for them (Ephesians 3:14-19). He prayed they would know God's will, be fruitful in ministry and strengthened by intimacy with God (Colossians 1:9-12). These apostolic prayers reflect a deeper dimension of prayers than most believers ever reach.

Apostolic prayers lay the foundation for the lives of people so that they will be able to do the work God called them to do and fulfill destiny. Apostles hear different messages by the Spirit. The revelation of the mystery of Christ is being revealed to the apostles and prophets (Ephesians 3:4-5).

Repeating Paul's prayers would be meaningless without the direction and anointing of the Spirit. If a person is led by the Spirit to pray some of the prayers Paul prayed, then these prayers would be effective today. However, it takes an apostle's insight and anointing to pray a true apostolic prayer. For example, believers could pray for a revelation of the knowledge of Jesus Christ and be on solid footing. However, such a prayer might not be the strategic prayer needed to mature believers and help them fulfill destiny. Only the Spirit can distinguish between a prayer that sounds good and a strategic prayer that will be effective and get results.

How Paul Taught Others to Pray

Paul's instructions on prayer are highlighted in the passage on prayer armor (Ephesians 6:10-20). The enemies of God's plan are spiritual, not human, and strategic prayers are aimed at spiritual enemies. Protection for the prayer warrior is provided by such elements of the armor as salvation, righteousness, truth, faith, and peace. The sword of the Spirit is the primary weapon used for both offense and defense. It can pierce through the heart of a matter and cut away things that bind up and hinder. Properly arrayed with armor and sword, the prayer warrior is prepared for all prayer and petition to pray at all times in the Spirit (Ephesians 6:18). Paul's reference to praying in the Spirit involves God's Spirit identifying what to pray and how to pray and the spirit man praying.

Paul wrote believers were to be devoted to prayer. "Devote yourselves to prayer, keeping alert in it with an attitude of thanksgiving" (Colossians 4:2). Being devoted to prayer involves seeking the Father's will, not trying to enforce your will. People cannot manipulate the Father in order to get the results from prayer which they want. Our God does not change, so he cannot be manipulated. The right kind of prayer changes things, not just any prayer.

Praying Strategically

The effective strategy in prayer is to glorify the Father. If you pray for needs to be met and are led by the needs, you will miss what glorifies the Father. The only way you know what glorifies the Father is to ask. The Spirit of God reveals the heart of God to his children (1 Corinthians 2:12). Listen to the Spirit and then pray as he guides you.

Strategic prayers align a believer's purpose with God's purpose. There are many plans in the heart of a person. Time and effort will be devoted to many of these plans, but not all of them will be successful. Applying faith to any of these plans will help make them more successful. Faith is a powerful force that can be used in fulfilling a person's plans and purpose.

The Father has prepared many good works for his children to accomplish, but they all require prayer to discover and fulfill. God created us to do the good things he already planned for us to do (Ephesians 2:10). These are the good works that will convince even the skeptics to glorify God (1 Peter 2:12). The carnal mind cannot understand such things, but believers can know these things by the Spirit. God's plans are most effective when he has someone to partner with him in implementing them. Partner with the Father in prayer by doing his will and fulfilling his purpose.

Here is an example to help you understand the concept of strategically praying by the Spirit. Suppose a man tells you he needs a job and asks for prayer. Many people would be quick to pray for a job for him. If you ask the Father how to pray, he may tell you to pray for this man's heart to be changed so he will become a good worker. The Father would know potential employers who want a good worker, but not a slothful worker. If you use your faith to get a job for a slothful worker, his new employer will not glorify God. If you pray for the man's heart to be changed so he will be a good worker, the employer will glorify God for the good worker. Using faith to manipulate situations is witchcraft. Stop manipulating situations. Instead, ask the Father for his guidance on prayers. Then your prayer will produce results and the Father will be glorified.

Personal Story on Strategic Prayers

Sherry and I minister to people in prisons and jails, and we know the hardships many of them face. Some of them ask for prayers to get out of prison or jail. In the past, we have reacted to their needs and prayed without knowing what the Lord was doing in their lives. Many people who are incarcerated get to the point where they turn their attention to the Lord and let him change their hearts and minds. The Lord told us to stop using our faith to get people out of prison or jail while he was still working on them there. Prayers are not to be used to control and manipulate situations. Pray for the Father's will to be done so he will be glorified.

The Challenge

Be devoted to strategic prayers that glorify God and get results.

Never take the easy way out by praying for the needs you see. Always ask for the Spirit's guidance on how to pray. He knows the future and what would glorify God. When the Spirit speaks to you, your faith will increase. That's the time to pray. When your prayers are guided by the Spirit, they will be effective.

How can you build a more productive prayer life to benefit the kingdom?

Chapter 11
STRATEGIC HEALING

Many people use medical and other natural means to combat the same sicknesses which Jesus overcame supernaturally. Medicine often deals only with symptoms, but Jesus dealt with the roots of sickness and got immediate results. Fighting sickness is a spiritual battle against spiritual forces. "We are fighting against the spiritual powers of evil in the heavenly places" (Ephesians 6:12 ERV). Believers have been given authority and power to heal the sick. In this chapter, you will learn about the Spirit's healing power and how to release it to overcome any sickness. Similar principles apply to other areas of life, as well.

Introducing Healing Power

The healing ministry of Jesus began after he was anointed with the power of the Spirit. God anointed Jesus with the Spirit's power to heal the sick (Acts 10:38). There was no sickness that he could not heal and no person too sick for him to heal. He even raised the dead (Luke 7:11-14, 8:49-56).

ENLIGHTENED AND EMPOWERED

Jesus gave authority over sickness and power to heal to his disciples (Luke 9:1-2). He told his disciples, "Heal the sick, raise the dead, cleanse the lepers, cast out demons" (Matthew 10:8). Peter and John healed a lame man outside the temple, explaining that it was not their own power but God's power that healed the man (Acts 3:1-16). When the people found out about the power of God operating in the lives of the apostles, they brought "people who were sick or afflicted with unclean spirits, and they were all being healed" (Acts 5:16).

Now, Jesus is giving the same authority over sickness and power to heal to all believers. After the resurrection, he said "All authority has been given to me in heaven and on earth" (Matthew 28:18). Jesus commissioned believers to heal the sick (Mark 16:14-18). The gospel of the kingdom will be proclaimed throughout the earth and demonstrated with healings, signs, and wonders.

The Spirit's healing power is given with measure to believers when they experience the new birth, and it increases when they are filled with the Spirit. Through the understanding of the power and guidance of the Spirit, believers can release the power to heal the sick.

Sherry and I were active in local congregations where people were saved, but other operations of the Spirit were practically non-existent. Those congregations prayed for God to heal sick people if it was his will without ever bothering to find out his will. These so-called prayers were filled with doubt and unbelief, so most of those people died without being healed. When our family needed healing, the Spirit led us to a place where the gifts of the Spirit operated and healings and miracles occurred. There we were taught about the operation of the Spirit. We were not able to operate in much authority until we found our ordained place in the body of Christ, having relationships with apostles and prophets. As our personal relationships with several apostles and prophets grew stronger so did our authority.

Taking Authority Over Sickness

Surrounded by sick and hurting people, Jesus said: "The blind receive sight, the lame walk, those who have leprosy are cleansed, the deaf hear, the dead are raised, and the good news is proclaimed to the poor" (Matthew 11:5 NIV). He was seeing into the supernatural realm by the eyes of the Spirit and speaking words of faith over the sick. By faith he only sees people healed and redeemed. His eyes "are too pure to look on evil" (Habakkuk 1:13 NIV).

The Spirit gives believers new eyes to see what Jesus sees. "Open the eyes of their hearts" (Ephesians 1:18 VOICE). Like Jesus, believers can see the people made whole through the eyes of the Spirit. See your own spirit, soul and body made whole, and it will help you see others made whole. By believing what Jesus did on the cross you will see the sick healed, and they will be healed.

It takes faith operating through believers for them to see the blind, deaf, lame and others made whole. By relying on what is seen through the eyes of the Spirit rather than natural sight, believers will be able to operate in the supernatural realm with authority and power. "We walk by faith, not by sight" (2 Corinthians 5:7). Believers have the ability to make people whole when they see and believe that they are made whole. If you believe, you will see people made whole.

Healing is in every believer just waiting to be activated. Faith releases that healing power in the person. Healing someone else helps fulfill his/her purpose and empowers you to fulfill yours. There are nine important approaches to healing, so it is critical to know from the Spirit which approaches are to be used for a particular individual. Using just one approach for every person will not work. An effective strategy for healing any person comes only from asking the Spirit for guidance.

Nine Ways to Release Healing Power

Jesus and the apostles demonstrated many different ways to release the Spirit's healing power. For example, Jesus healed those who were blind by touching some blind eyes, spitting on others, and anointing others with mud (Matthew 9:27-31; Mark 8:22-25; John 9:1-7). Inquire of the Lord to find out which approach is needed to heal each sick person. There is always a way for healing, and that way is the strategic approach. It is the only way that will work. Only the Spirit knows which approach will work for a particular sick person. Nine important ways to release the Spirit's healing power are discussed below.

1. Releasing Faith for Healing

With faith, anyone can be healed. "All things are possible to him who believes" (Mark 9:23). Jesus told several of the people who were healed that their faith healed them. The woman who had been subject to bleeding for twelve years was healed by her faith (Mark 5:34). Blind Bartimaeus received sight by his faith (Mark 10:52).

When Sherry and I first began learning about God's healing ways, we had no basis for faith in healing. We needed to study God's word on healing and surround ourselves with people who believed in healing. Also, we immersed ourselves in teachings about healing. Then our faith in the area of healing began to grow. Faith comes by hearing God's word (Romans 10:17). We would listen to teaching tapes and scripture tapes all night long. It took a period of several months for our faith in healing to become strong. Then we prayed for healing and believed in the Spirit's healing power. We have been healed and our children have been healed over and over again.

2. Calling on the Name of Jesus

Faith in the name of Jesus heals the sick. Peter told a lame man who had never walked "In the name of Jesus Christ of Nazareth, walk" (Acts 3:6). He told a man who was paralyzed

"Aeneas, Jesus Christ heals you; get up and make your bed" (Acts 9:34). Both of these men were healed immediately by using the name of Jesus. The name of Jesus carried such power that the disciples were forbidden to preach in that name by the religious people (Acts 5:28). When Phillip preached Christ and the name of Jesus, many were saved, healed and received miracles (Acts 8:4-13). There is no name higher than the name of Jesus (Philippians 2:9-11). Trust in his name to release healing power. There is supernatural power in the name of Jesus.

3. Praying for the Sick

The prayer of faith releases the Spirit's power to heal the sick. "The prayer offered in faith will restore the one who is sick, and the Lord will raise him up" (James 5:15). We frequently pray for those who are sick and have seen many people healed from these prayers. The spirit of intercession may come upon us to pray for the healing of others. We intercede until we know the victory has come and healing has been released. The victory may come in an hour or so; but when we are responding to the spirit of intercession, we always experience victory in the supernatural realm.

Sherry and I have learned to be vessels for the Lord's use in intercession. The spirit of intercession often flows through us to bring forth God's purposes on the earth. I once interceded for a woman whom I had not heard from for several months.

As I was interceding, she was battling for her life in another state. Her spirit left her body and began traveling through a tunnel with a light at the end of it. Before she reached the end of the tunnel the Lord told her to return to the earth for her purpose here had not ended. Then the spirit of intercession lifted from me, and I knew in my spirit she had the victory. Later her husband confirmed she died that night but was revived. She continued to preach the gospel and heal the sick.

The prayer of agreement is especially effective in releasing the healing power. "If two of you agree on earth about anything that they may ask, it shall be done for them by my Father who is in heaven" (Matthew 18:19). It is good for the sick person to agree with those who are praying for him/her.

4. Anointing the Sick

Anoint the sick with oil and they will be healed. The disciples cast out demons and anointed the sick with oil and healed them (Mark 6:13). Those who are sick are to call for the elders who will pray over them and anoint them with oil to be healed (James 5:14-15). The anointing oil is a point of contact that helps people release their faith to be healed.

Pieces of cloth can be anointed as a store of healing power. Then the pieces of cloth can be used when needed or sent to the sick for deliverance and healing. When handkerchiefs and aprons anointed by Paul were placed on sick people, the diseases and evil spirits left them (Acts 19:11-12). We have given anointed handkerchiefs to sick people in many countries and have received glorious reports of God's healing power.

5. Laying Hands on the Sick

Believers carry healing power in their hands and release it when they lay hands on the sick. Near Bethsaida, Jesus twice laid his hands on the eyes of a blind man and his sight was restored (Mark 8:22-26). Believers "will lay hands on the sick, and they will recover" (Mark 16:18). We lay hands on the sick as the Spirit guides us to do so. It would be inappropriate to lay hands on someone who first needs deliverance from a demon, so we pray beforehand. We have seen many people healed by laying our hands on them. Sherry and I lay hands on ourselves and on each other when we need healing. Everyone needs people of faith around them who can lay hands on them when they are sick.

6. Giving Spiritual Gifts to the Sick

Gifts of the Spirit are manifested for people to help each other. Paul identifies nine gifts of the Spirit (1 Corinthians 12:1-11). Any of these gifts can be used in healing, but the power gifts of faith, healing and miracles are most prominent in healing. Sherry operates in all three of these power gifts, and we have seen many people healed as we operate in the gifts.

The gift of knowledge is often given to help people understand how the gifts are flowing at a particular time. For example, the Spirit may reveal that the Lord is healing backs or hearts. Whoever responds to this word of knowledge can receive their healing. The word of wisdom may give people understanding and direction for being healed. Discerning of spirits operates to show when demons need to be cast out in order for someone to be healed.

7. Speaking the Word to Heal the Sick

Speaking words of faith to sickness will make it leave a person. If you believe without any doubt in your heart, you can speak faith and have whatever you say (Mark 11:23). Sometimes we send the word of faith to heal those who are not present with us. We may know by a telephone call or by the Spirit someone needs healing, so we speak healing to them. Many have been healed by sending God's word to them (Psalm 107:20).

8. Stopping the Reaping of Iniquities

Sin has consequences. The payment of sin is death (Romans 6:23). Hosea referred to the consequences of sin as the reaping of iniquities (Hosea 10:13). The consequences of sin may be passed down from one generation to the next. "As for those who are not loyal to me, their children will endure the consequences of their sins for three or four generations" (Exodus 20:5 VOICE). Such consequences are called generational curses. Some sins and generational curses open the doors for sickness and hinder a person's receiving the Spirit's healing power. Repentance is the cure for sin and generational curses. On the cross, Jesus purchased redemption from the curse of the law for all (Galatians 3:13). Stopping the reaping of iniquities requires a person to recognize, believe and acknowledge the redemptive work of Jesus on the cross.

When I learned to release the Spirit's healing power, I was able to pray and receive healing for my children. When one child reached the age of accountability, I prayed like before, but he got sicker. When I inquired of the Lord, I discovered he had been involved in sin. I addressed the sin problem with my child and led him to repentance. Then and only then could he receive his healing. If something is blocking your healing, inquire of the Lord and follow his guidance to be healed.

9. Casting Demons out of the Sick

Some people need deliverance from demonic forces in order to be healed. Jesus gave his disciples "authority over unclean spirits, to cast them out, and to heal every kind of disease and every kind of sickness" (Matthew 10:1). A person controlled by demons may lack the faith to be healed on his/her own, so approaches other than just faith may be needed. The gift of discerning of spirits is often manifested before we know a person needs to be delivered from evil spirits in order to be healed.

Sherry prayed for a woman on her deathbed and saw a large reptile-like demon which was trying to kill her. She cast the demon out, and the woman was healed. Soon we heard the woman was serving the Lord and teaching his word.

With each approach, it is important for those believers who minister healing to others to be covered with the blood of Jesus. They can be covered with his blood by believing and acknowledging the work which Jesus did on the cross. There is great power and protection in his blood when it is activated.

Believe and Receive the Healing Power

Many who long to be healed do not understand that they have a critical role in the healing process. In order for the sick to be healed, they have to believe Jesus is able to heal them and receive the healing power when it is released to them. Two blind men who desired to be healed followed Jesus, asking for healing mercy (Matthew 9:27-31). Before healing them, Jesus asked whether they believed he was able to heal them. They believed, and they were healed by their faith. The centurion's servant was healed by faith (Matthew 8:5-13). Jesus told a leper who desired to be healed, "Stand up and go; your faith has made you well" (Luke 17:19). Even Jesus was not able to heal the sick in the midst of doubt and unbelief. Jesus could not do any mighty works in his hometown because of their unbelief (Mark 6:5-6).

The healing power is not to be wasted by letting it fall to the ground, but it is to be actively received by those who desire to be healed. "The power of the Lord was with Jesus to heal the sick" (Luke 5:17 NIV). When a woman touched the robe which Jesus was wearing, the healing power went out from him to heal her (Mark 5:25-34). Receive the power to be healed.

Even when a person is healed, there is still a battle to be fought. We have seen several people let family, friends, and doctors talk them out of their healing. The enemy comes to steal a person's healing. Lying symptoms may remain. Stand by faith and be ready to defend your healing by speaking out and acting on God's word.

Personal Story on Strategic Healing

A woman came to Sherry after a morning teaching session in Mexico and asked her to pray over the lumps in her body. Sherry asked if she could first seek the Lord to find out what he would have her do, and the woman agreed. When she prayed, the Lord told her to hit the woman in the chest three times and the lumps would be gone. When the people came back together after lunch, Sherry called for the woman to come forward. She said she was going to hit her three times in the chest. The woman agreed that Sherry could hit her. Then Sherry hit her hard three times in the chest, and the woman fell down on the floor and looked dead. After a while, she was helped to her seat. Then we saw her get up and go to the restroom. The woman testified that she went to the restroom where she passed a ball of blood and the three lumps left her body. The Spirit knew what needed to be done for the woman to be healed.

The Challenge

Let God's healing power flow through you every day.
Believe God for your own healing and opportunities to bring healing to others. God's healing power is stronger than any sickness. No person is too sick or too far gone for you to minister healing. Never back down from sickness nor give in to sickness. Man does not know a better way to heal than God, so ask for his guidance. Let the Spirit guide you on how to release the healing power strategically.

What hinders you from being healed and made whole in your spirit, soul, and body?

Chapter 12
WALK IN THE SPIRIT

You can have what you see. So, what do you see? If you look only at natural and mundane things, those are what you will have. If you look into the supernatural realm, you will have God's supernatural power to change natural things and receive the things from heaven. God promised Abraham he could have what he saw. "All the land which you see, I will give it to you and to your descendants forever" (Genesis 13:15). When Abraham looked around and saw trouble on every side, he looked up and saw Jesus. Jesus said, "Abraham rejoiced to see my day, and he saw it and was glad" (John 8:56). The Spirit gives believers spiritual eyes to see the supernatural realm. Those who receive new life from the Spirit are to follow the Spirit; "If we live by the Spirit, let us also walk by the Spirit" (Galatians 5:25). In this chapter, you will discover how to operate in the supernatural realm and do things which seem to be impossible. Walk in the spirit and shift the atmosphere wherever you go. The light and power enable you to change things.

Introducing the Supernatural Realm

The world has two realities: natural and supernatural. "Faith is the assurance of things you have hoped for, the absolute conviction that there are realities you've never seen" (Hebrews 11:1 VOICE). The term supernatural means beyond natural. The two realities can be contrasted as the seen and the unseen. The supernatural is the side of reality where God is unseen by those on the natural side. Yet, God lived in the natural as the man Jesus. He operated in the supernatural as he calmed the sea, walked on water, raised the dead, etc. Jesus brought the supernatural into the natural and gave the supernatural its meaning for believers. The supernatural is another side of the same world which operates by natural laws.

The heroes of faith did impossible things by the power of God as examples for believers to follow today. Moses stretched forth his staff to part the Red Sea so the Israelites could escape from Pharaoh's army (Exodus 14:21-22). The Israelites blew trumpets and shouted to destroy the great wall around Jericho (Joshua 6:20). Sick people were laid in the streets where Peter walked so his shadow would fall on some and heal them (Acts 5:15-16). When Paul and Silas prayed and praised God in prison, all the prison doors flew open, and everyone's chains came loose (Acts 16:25-26). These heroes operated by faith in the supernatural realm. Believers today can operate in faith in the supernatural realm to do impossible things. "All things are possible to him who believes" (Mark 9:23).

The Spirit bypasses the natural mind and its operations. He gives believers the ability to see into the supernatural realm. "Stephen, full of the Holy Spirit, looked up to heaven and saw the glory of God and Jesus standing at the right hand of God" (Acts 7:55 NIV). John saw a door standing open in heaven and heard a voice say, "Come up here, and I will show you what must take place after these things" (Revelation 4:1). The Spirit was inviting John into the supernatural realm where he would see things to come.

The supernatural realm is beyond faith. Seeing into the supernatural realm is different from seeing something that does not exist by faith. Paul prayed for believers which already possessed faith to have their spiritual eyes opened (Ephesians 1:16-19). Faith sees things that are not, but eyes of the Spirit see things which already exist in the supernatural realm. The things which exist in the supernatural realm can be brought into the natural realm by following the Spirit and speaking faith-filled words.

Doing what the Spirit directs you to do is a supernatural action. Whatever you have can be turned into something supernatural by following the Spirit. God's power is released by supernatural actions. Supernatural actions receive supernatural rewards (Matthew 5:44-47). "He who receives a prophet in the name of a prophet shall receive a prophet's reward; and he who receives a righteous man in the name of a righteous man shall receive a righteous man's reward"

(Matthew 10:41). Operating in the supernatural realm, believers are able to do things which are impossible in the natural.

Do Seven Impossible Things

Like Jesus, believers can do impossible things by following the Spirit. There is no limit on how many impossible things a believer can do, but here is a list of the most important ones. Begin with these seven impossible things, and you will be able to fulfill God's purpose.

1. Love like Jesus Loves

Jesus loved his disciples by teaching them, guiding them, and serving them. He demonstrated the greatest love by sacrificing his life on the cross. Jesus told the disciples "This is my commandment, that you love one another, just as I have loved you" (John 15:12). Those who believe in Jesus can love because he first loved them. The standard for love is no longer to love others as you love yourself, but it is to love as you have been loved. You can love your enemies with the love of Jesus.

2. Pray Constantly

Jesus comes again suddenly, so believers are always to be praying. Many people consider their prayer time to be limited by activities such as eating, talking or sleeping, but there are no such limitations in the supernatural realm. Paul wrote, "Pray without ceasing" (1 Thessalonians 5:17). You can pray constantly in the supernatural realm because your spirit never sleeps. It is always ready to pray.

3. Worship Inwardly and in Harmony with the Heavenly Host

When an angel announced the birth of Jesus, "there appeared with the angel a multitude of the heavenly host praising God" (Luke 2:8-13). The heavenly host is always praising the Lord. Let heaven and earth praise the Lord (Psalm 148:1-14). The heavenly host praises God in spirit and in truth as a vast multitude of true worshipers. "True worshipers will worship the Father in spirit and truth" (John 4:23). All true worshipers worship the same way and in harmony with each other.

God is a spirit, so believers connect with him in the spirit and through his Spirit. True worship is an inward expression of the heart, not an outward expression of playing musical instruments, singing or dancing. Abraham used the term worship to describe obedience, not music (Genesis 22:5). Music may help create an atmosphere for true worshipers to express themselves from their hearts. When you are filled with the Spirit, you are empowered to "sing and make music with your hearts attuned to God" (Ephesians 5:19 VOICE). The melody in your heart will be as acceptable and pleasing to God as music is to us. Without your affections and inward melody of the heart, no external music can be pleasing to his ear. By following the Spirit believers can worship inwardly and in harmony with the heavenly host in the supernatural realm.

4. Heal the Sick

Motivated by compassion, Jesus preached the gospel of the kingdom and demonstrated the gospel by healing the sick. Jesus gave his disciples "authority over unclean spirits, to cast them out, and to heal every kind of disease and every kind of sickness" (Matthew 10:1). Believers can follow the Spirit to heal the sick. The approach may vary, but healing is always the result for those who follow the Spirit and operate in the supernatural realm.

5. Remove All Obstacles

Jesus destroyed an unproductive fig tree as a warning for those who would hinder God's people. Whoever trusts God without any doubt can speak to a mountain and cause it to be removed (Mark 11:23). The hindrances which need to be removed out of a believer's life include fear, doubt, and unbelief. The Spirit shows believers how to remove any hindrance so they can walk in victory.

6. Set aside Your Rights and Interests to Do God's Will

Even though Jesus has always been God, he laid down his glory and majesty to come to earth and die on the cross. Jesus said,

"If anyone wishes to come after me, he must deny himself, and take up his cross and follow me" (Matthew 16:24). In the natural, it is impossible for people to deny their own rights and interests, but the Spirit helps believers submit to the Father's will. Those who follow the Spirit and operate in the supernatural realm are true disciples.

7. Do the Mighty Works of Jesus and Greater Works

Jesus did mighty works to demonstrate his relationship with the Father. Now believers can do mighty works to demonstrate their relationships with the Father, his Son, and his Spirit. Jesus said, "Anyone who believes in me will do the same works I have done, and even greater works because I am going to be with the Father" (John 14:12). Nothing is impossible for those who believe and follow the Spirit.

Personal Story about the Supernatural Realm

Sherry saw a vision of her ministering to a young woman with a heart problem. In the vision, she laid on top of the young woman and God healed her heart. Then the young woman got up and began to leap up and down. That night at the service, she saw the young woman and called her up on the platform. Someone had to help her walk because she was unable to breathe properly. Then Sherry acted on the vision which she had seen earlier. She instructed the young woman to lie down on the platform and she did. In front of all the people, Sherry laid on the young woman as she had seen in the vision and God's power went out of her into the young woman. The young woman was totally healed, got up and began to leap and dance.

The Challenge

Be the expression of Christ in your world by speaking his words and doing his works and greater works.
Do not limit yourself, because God has pulled off the limits. Nothing is impossible to those who believe. You can do whatever you see with your spiritual eyes. Follow the Spirit to bring the finished work of the cross out of the supernatural realm into the natural realm by your faith, words, and actions. Do the impossible!

What impossible things do you need to do in order to fulfill destiny?

Chapter 13
CONCLUSIONS

The Spirit enlightens and empowers believers to soar to new heights. Only through the Spirit can you move higher in the things of the Lord. In this chapter, you will discover where you are on the journey of discovery and personal growth and what direction to move. It is presented as a guide to help you identify where you are on the journey and what areas in your life need to be strengthened. As you read the chapter, ask the Lord for guidance by his Spirit into your destiny.

Discover the Light and Power

When God's Spirit breathes life into people, their spirits are made alive and the supernatural realm opens up to them. They become spirit beings and move like the wind which brings freedom. They are free to follow the Spirit and seek heavenly things which were unimaginable before the new birth.

Study God's word yourself and build a relationship with his Spirit who is your teacher and guide. These efforts will help protect you from deceptions and limitations in life. You will be able to discover divine purpose and appropriate God's promises. Stay free like the wind!

Inside every believer, there is a desire to know about God and to be close to him. When a believer is first born again the desire for God is like a flame. The more believers release to God, the more they become aware of his Spirit and spiritual things. They remain limited and powerless until they are filled with the Spirit. When they are immersed in the Spirit and fire, the flame within becomes a roaring fire that fuels desires for the things of God and burns up things of the enemy. Being filled with the Spirit opens the spiritual realm and unlimited power to believers.

God's word exhorts believers to be filled with the Spirit and to pray in the new tongues of their spirit language. The Spirit leads believers to the truth and the deep things of God one step at a time. His power helps them confront difficult situations.

Knowing how to hear the Spirit's voice is important in order to follow him. He does not speak like a man. His words are supernatural and contain boundless energy. He speaks on a frequency which is not heard by the natural ear. Instead, his words are heard by the spirit man. Tuning the spiritual ear to his frequency requires spiritual growth. Staying tuned to his frequency involves a lifestyle committed to the Lord. The Spirit uses different tones of voice to correct, comfort and guide. Stay tuned to his frequency and listen closely to changes in the tone of his voice.

CONCLUSIONS

Draw on the Light and Power

Are you bearing fruit which lasts? God's kingdom is built by fruit bearers producing a bountiful harvest of everlasting fruit. The kingdom is full of fruit bearers and only fruit bearers. Others may see the kingdom and even enter it for a time, but no one can remain in the kingdom for long without bearing fruit. Recognize the critical role you have in the kingdom and begin visualizing yourself as a fruit bearer making a difference in this world.

A sense of wonder helps believers stay sensitive to the anointing dwelling within them. While the strongest and wisest believers may miss the subtle witness of the anointing, the child and those with childlike faith have a simplicity and spontaneity which helps them quickly respond to the anointing. The anointing is an important guide because it gives a believer the assurance that God's will is always available. Also, the anointing within is always available for ministry to others.

Your response to the inward witness of the anointing is important. Denying and ignoring the anointing will cause its witness within to diminish. If your response reflects a sense of wonder, you will ignite a supernatural fire within you and become more sensitive to the anointing. Be quick to act on the anointing, and its role in your life will become greater.

As believers mature in the Lord, they are able to walk in more of his authority and power. Spiritual maturity requires a believer to trust God's word and have strong relationships with the Spirit and his/her ordained spiritual father. The Spirit's light and power are especially important in spiritual maturity because these are the growth elements. Without both light and power, a believer cannot grow spiritually and become like Christ.

God has a spiritual father for every son (neither male nor female) to help lead him to maturity. Spiritual fathers impart things to their spiritual sons that cannot be gotten any other way. By joining yourself to the spiritual father which God ordained for you, you will be able to mature spiritually and fulfill your own destiny. Identify and join with those God has ordained as your own spiritual sons. Invest time and effort in your spiritual sons, and then release them into their destiny.

God's grace flows through relationships between God and believers and among believers. A relationship with God is a conduit for the flow of his grace. Humility enhances the flow of grace in relationships and results in blessings and growth.

Relationships are highly valued in God's kingdom because God uses them in his building. The new structure of the church is built upon those relationships ordained by God. Physical buildings hinder the process of developing strong personal relationships. The growth of God occurs only in ordained relationships called grace joints. Life pulsating through relationships is the very heartbeat of the kingdom. The power and authority of God's kingdom flow through grace joints.

CONCLUSIONS

One of the most important things you can do in this life is to build strong personal relationships. Seek God's grace and you will find it in abundance and be able to minister grace to others through personal relationships. As you give grace to others, you will receive more grace. Take advantage of opportunities to fellowship with others, because they can lead to new and/or stronger relationships. Be led by the Spirit in investing time and effort in personal relationships. Invest wisely in those relationships which lift up Jesus Christ in you and in others.

Demonstrate the Light and Power

Everyone can offer himself/herself to be used as a vessel through which spiritual gifts flow. A person can seek the Lord to identify his/her own calling and gifts. Spiritual relationships can help identify and confirm a person's calling and gifts. Spiritual gifts are received by faith and operated by faith.

Opportunities to be used of God exist everywhere. As believers make themselves aware of the supernatural realm and the things which God will do through them, they can be used to advance God's kingdom. Those who earnestly pursue spiritual gifts will be a blessing to others and fulfill their own calling.

Seek to glorify the Father with your prayers. Be led by the Spirit rather than by the needs of people. Prayers are most effective when they relate to God's interests and concerns for others. Hear what the Father says by his Spirit and speak it into the earth. Pray what you hear the Father say, so your prayers will be strategic and effective.

Healing was purchased by the precious blood of Jesus on the cross, so it's always God's will to heal every sick person. All believers have authority over sickness and the power to heal the sick. Healing demonstrates God's kingdom, draws the lost to Jesus, and strengthens believers for the journey.

There are a variety of approaches to healing, ranging from laying hands on the sick to casting demons out of them. The strategic approach to healing, which comes from inquiring of the Lord and following his Spirit, will always be effective. The Spirit searches the heart of the all-knowing God to find healing for each and every sickness. By following the guidance of the Spirit, believers apply strategic healing to the sick and see them healed.

You are the light of the world. Is the Spirit's light flowing through you to reach the lost, encourage the downcast and strengthen believers? You have access to tremendous light and power, but they have to be received and released to make a difference in this world. Let nothing hinder or limit you. Do things that seem to be impossible to the carnal mind. Walk in the spirit and shift the atmosphere wherever you go. Destiny is your reward.

NOTES

A Request for Your Review

Please leave a review of this book at Amazon, Barnes and Noble or some other major book distributor.

Our Other Books

Prophetic Voice Rising: Releasing the Gift

This book will help develop the gifts of prophets, seers, intercessors and psalmists. Also, it will help anyone prophesy.

Marriage by the Spirit: Rhythms of Grace

Find fulfillment and joy in marriage by following the Holy Spirit. This book offers a fresh approach to marriage.

Walking in the Father's Riches

Are you facing financial problems? This book is a lifeline for those seeking the way out of their financial problems.

Contact Us on the Web

www.FredAndSherryWhite.com

CPSIA information can be obtained
at www.ICGtesting.com
Printed in the USA
FFOW03n1113250218
45245353-45851FF

9 780982 613559